walks in mysterious wales

Laurence Main

Published by Sigma Leisure – an imprint of
Sigma Press, 1 South Oak Lane, Wilmslow, Cheshire SK9 6AR, England.

British Library Cataloguing in Publication Data
A CIP record for this book is available from the British Library.

ISBN: 1-85058-368-4

Typesetting and Design by: Sigma Press, Wilmslow, Cheshire.

Cover photograph: The Summer Solstice sunset from Carningli, Pembrokeshire, overlooking Dinas Head.

Maps: Perrott Cartographics

Photographs: The author

Printed by: MFP Print & Design

preface

This is a book of walks in Wales, averaging five miles in length, from and to places which represent the great store of legend, magic, mystery and sense of belonging to the living land that is still so obvious to the interested observer fresh from the dormant countryside on the eastern side of Offa's Dyke. It has two aims. One is to open the eyes of the walker to the nature of the land he or she sets foot on, so that mutual love can be exchanged and humankind shakes itself awake to the need to live in harmony with Mother Earth. The other is to invite those armchair followers of the New Age fashion and even those most worthy souls who tend their organic or veganic gardens to embrace a little bit more of the planet, to let their soft feet inform remote areas that they are not neglected and to allow places where the spirit has survived more strongly to work through us.

None of these walks involves more than even nine miles, but there are strenuous mountain climbs to give the toughest a sense of satisfaction. Cadair Idris reaches up to 2928 feet, while Bannau Sir Gaer, above Llyn y Fan Fach, is an impressive 2457 feet. The usual rules of walking in the hills apply. Check the weather forecast, take the required Ordnance Survey Pathfinder or Outdoor Leisure (1: 25,000 scale) maps and a good compass and know how to use them, wear good walking boots, carry spare clothing, including an anorak, remember a torch and batteries but don't start out so late that you end up walking in the dark, while a little reserve of food and drink is always welcome.

Some of these walks are difficult to get to without a car but whenever public transport is available please make the effort to use it. The motorcar is one of the chief enemies of the living earth and it makes a nonsense of your reverence for nature if you add to the pollution and demand for more roads. The local bus or train will be glad of your support. If using it means staying away for the odd night, welcome that as a bonus, an opportunity to pitch your tent in a beautiful, peaceful spot or to meet new friends at a youth hostel or bed and breakfast.

The list of walks in this book is neither comprehensive nor representative. In fact, it is merely the tip of a huge iceberg. Taste these samples and you could be feasting from the Welsh landscape for a lifetime. Go in the spirit of love and you will receive much from it.

When I wasn't using public transport, I was very grateful for the following people who drove me to the starts of some walks and sometimes accompanied me along the routes: Beck Cunningham, Emma Orbach, Letty Rowan, Jeff Loo, George Wemyss and the Rev. Jim McKnight. There was also a Thelma who spent one night on top of Carningli with me and drove me to the Llanbrynmair walk. I may have forgotten the surname but I'll remember your free spirit.

Laurence Main

contents

the walks

LOCATION MAP

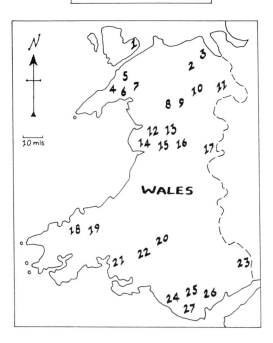

N

10 mls

WALES

Introduction

The spirit of the landscape is still very close to the surface in Wales. Look and you may see yourself standing under it, an integral part of nature. Know this land and you realise that we do not possess it; the land possesses us. Places can be sacred, of spiritual importance, as part of the divine plan. They retain a memory of the past, so that we can join with John Masefield in feeling "the hillside thronged by souls unseen/ Who knew the interest in me, and were keen/ That man alive should understand man dead."

The Preselis, for example, have an innate holiness that puts any cathedral, mosque or temple in its place. Try to find a more moving church than the one that St. Brynach was guided to found at Nevern. Carningli is the holy hill where the saint received his vision of a white sow giving birth at Nevern. What more potent symbol could there be of the bountiful Earth Goddess with her many teats, the provider of all her babies' wants? It is connected to the peak by a ley or spirit path, to the very spot where St. Brynach saw angels ascending the stairway to heaven.

The Underworld

Carningli is also the gateway to hell, or, rather, the Annwn of the Celts. This Underworld includes the realm of the fairies and there's no better place to go looking for them than on the slopes of Frenni Fawr.

Entrances to Annwn are everywhere. It seems an easy place to drop into but how about getting out again? Taliesin tells us in his 'Spoils of Annwn' how Arthur descended into the Underworld

to rescue Gweir (Man) and carry off the inspirational and rejuvenating cauldron of the Goddess Ceridwen. Make a pilgrimage to
Llandderfel, where one of Arthur's knights and a hero of the Battle
of Camlan, fought at Dinas Mawddwy, also managed to find his
way out of hell and to bring others out with him.

Is this 'the land in the west, among mountains of gold, silver,
iron and tin' that the apocryphal Book of Enoch consigns the
fallen angels and the men they had led astray to? Is not Idris the
Arab name for Enoch and is not Cadair Idris buzzed by the
Hounds of the Underworld? Was not Mount Ida to the Greeks and
Trojans the mount of Ideas? Spend a night at the summit of Cadair
Idris and will you not become an inspired poet, if you survive
death or madness? The mystical Book of Enoch was avidly read
by the early Gnostic Christians. What was the original Celtic
Church? Legend suggests that its inspiration came direct from
Jesus and the Holy Land, rather than from the imperial bureau-
crats of Rome.

Witchcraft and folklore

Bring some garlic with you when walking around Llanddona, for
this is witch country. Things are safer in Denbigh now that the
dragon has been disposed of, although the life story of Henry
Morton Stanley is an object lesson in what can happen to you if
you are born on a dragon line or ley. If you do lose your head you
could always have it restored in the healing waters of Holywell.

There was no refuge for the traitor Vortigern at Nant
Gwrtheyrn, but he shouldn't have tried to sacrifice Myrddin at
Dinas Emrys. Punishment by flooding engulfed Tegid's Bala and
Cantre'r Gwaelod, so it's worth knowing of sanctuaries 'beyond
the billow', as at Darowen. This is marked by a triangle of
standing stones. On the hill above Llanbrynmair the stones
ringed the shamanic ox-hide at a place of visions.

Cast your bread upon the waters of Llyn y Fan Fach and you
may end up marrying a fairy princess. Treat her kindly or she'll

return to where she came from. This rule even applies to fairy cows, as the farmer at Dysyrnant found out at Cwm Maethlon. White ladies can also bring treasure, as at Ogmore, while I know someone who received a vision of the Goddess in her hag aspect in the cave at Carreg Cennen. If you meet a white lady without a head, help her to find it, as someone did for poor Gwenllian at Kidwelly.

Ley lines and dowsing

This world is unfair, as John Newton Davies of Montgomery could vouch for, but his grave did remain bare for more than the required generation and his soul may have had a direct link with the nearest holy hill. Spirit paths are everywhere. Even the first modern cremation took place on one, but then the druid tradition has always been kept alive in Wales.

Much primary research remains to be done on leys but a small band of dedicated people keep adding to our knowledge. Join them and support them by subscribing to 'The Ley Hunter' magazine, P.O. Box 92, Penzance, Cornwall, TR18 2XL. You may be able to piece together this jigsaw by preserving vital local knowledge and informing others of it. I'd love to know where Moel Lladdfa, Fronguddio and Y Bedren are, for example. I asked and checked my maps when in Llangar but couldn't find them. Now, if they fell in a straight line with All Saints' Church, that would be interesting.

Whilst dowsing at Valle Crucis Abbey I did meet somebody with local knowledge. The CADW lady was none other than the daughter of S.G. Wildman, the author of 'The Blackhorse Men'. I'd just dowsed a line that led to nothing of significance on the map but she remembered her father being sure that a cross had once been carved on that particular hillside.

The Welsh Language

You won't get full value from the Welsh countryside without some knowledge of the Welsh language, so here are some Welsh pronunciations, words and phrases:

Pronunciation

a   = ah

c   = k (hard)

ch = as in loch

dd = th in the

e   = eh

f   = v

ff = f

g   = as in go (hard)

ngh = as in anguish

i   = ee

ll = say l, keep tongue in this position and gently blow

o   = oh

th = as in through (not as in the)

w   = often as oo, with cwm (valley) sounding as coomb

y   = as e in the (y or yr), or as i, so that *Dyffryn* sounds like *derffrin*

There are mutations in Welsh, making Llanberis the sacred enclosure (llan) of Peris (p mutates to b). Similarly Llanbedr refers to St Peter (Pedr).

Common words

The following is a list of the most common words you are likely to find on Ordnance Survey maps and other documents. They can often be recognised as parts of compound words, for example as in Llyn Cwmffynnon, the name of a small lake in Snowdonia.

aber	= estuary, river-mouth or confluence
afon	= river
bach, fach	= small
bedd	= grave
betws	= chapel or oratory
blaen	= head of the valley
bont, pont	= bridge
braich	= arm
brith	= speckled
bryn	= hill
bwlch	= pass, defile
bychan	= little
cadair	= chair
cae	= field
caer	= fort
capel	= chapel
carn, carnedd	= pile of stones
carreg	= rock
castell	= castle
cau	= deep hollow
cefn	= ridge
celli, gelli	= grove
ceunant	= ravine
clogwyn	= precipice
coch	= red
coed	= woodland

congl	= corner
cors, gors	= bog
craig	= rock
crib	= narrow ridge
croes	= cross
cwm	= cirque, valley
dinas	= fort
dol, ddol	= meadow
drws	= door
dwr	= water
dwy	= two
dyffryn	= valley
eglwys	= church
eira	= snow
esgair	= mountain shoulder
fawr, mawr	= big
felin, melin	= mill
ffordd	= road
ffridd	= mountain pasture
ffynnon	= well, spring
foel, moel	= rounded hill
fynydd, mynydd	= mountain
gam	= crooked
glan	= bank, shore
glas, las	= blue, green
glyder	= heap
glyn	= glen
gwastad	= plain, level ground
gwern	= marsh
gwyn	= white
gwynt	= wind

hafod, hafotty	=	summer dwelling
hen	=	old
hendre	=	winter dwelling
hir	=	long
isa, isaf	=	lower
llan	=	sacred enclosure, church
llechwedd	=	hillside
llethr	=	slope
llwyd	=	grey
llwyn	=	grove
llyn	=	lake
maen	=	stone
maes	=	field
morfa	=	coastal marsh
mur	=	wall
nant	=	brook, stream
newydd	=	new
oer	=	cold
ogof	=	cave
oleu	=	light
pant	=	small hollow
pen	=	head, top
penrhyn	=	promontory
pentre, pentref	=	village
pistyll	=	spout, cataract
plas	=	mansion
pwll	=	pool
rhaeadr	=	waterfall
rhiw	=	hill
rhos	=	moorland, marsh
rhyd	=	ford

ucha, uchaf	= upper
uwch	= above
waun	= moor
y	= the, of the
yn	= in
ynys	= island
ysgol	= school, ladder
ysgubor	= barn
ystrad	= valley floor, strath
sarn	= paved way, causeway
sych	= dry
tal	= end
tan	= under
tarren	= hill
tir	= land
tomen	= mound
traeth	= stretch of shore
tre	= town, hamlet
tri	= three
trwyn	= nose, promontory
twll	= hole
ty	= house
tyddyn	= smallholding

If you can say nothing else, do try this:

| Good morning | = Bore da (bor-eh-da) |
| Thank you | = diolch (dee-olc) |

'Llwybr Cyhoeddus' is Welsh for 'public footpath'

The Ramblers

Each walk in this book follows rights of way to which you, as a member of the public, have unrestricted access, or agreed courtesy paths where dogs are not allowed. Should you come across any problems, send full details (including grid references) to: The Ramblers in Wales, Ty'r Cerddwyr, High Street, Gresford, Wrexham, Clwyd, LL12 8PT; telephone 01978 855148. Better still, join the Ramblers, go out on their group walks and volunteer to help deal with path problems yourself.

The Country Code

☐ Guard against all risk of fire

☐ Fasten all gates (NB this is the official advice. In practice, sheep farmers usually leave gates open on purpose so that sheep can reach water etc, so 'leave gates as you find them')

☐ Keep dogs under proper control

☐ Avoid damaging fences, hedges and walls

☐ Keep to paths across farmland

☐ Leave no litter

☐ Safeguard water supplies

☐ Protect wildlife, wild plants and trees

☐ Go carefully on country roads

☐ Respect the life of the countryside

Get to the walks by public transport!

1. Llanɔɔonɑ

Route: Llanddona – St. Dona's Church – Bwrdd Arthur – Llanddona.

Distance: 5 miles. Moderate.

Maps: OS Pathfinders 751 Bangor & Llangefni and 735 Red Wharf Bay.

Start: The Owain Glyndŵr Inn, Llanddona (SH 576797).

Access: Llanddona is on a minor road north-west of Beaumaris on the Isle of Anglesey. Bus no. 53 connects it with Bangor, where there is a railway station. Telephone 01286 679535 for times.

The Witches of Llanddona

This area is natural witch country, for its parish church is dedicated to St. Dona, who must be the Christian form of the Earth Goddess of that name. Celtic myth states that Don was the wife of Llyr, whose son Bran was the ally of Joseph of Arimathea and the chief agent for the introduction of Christianity to Britain. Her territory was protected by the hill fort known as Bwrdd Arthur, one of many candidates for King Arthur's Round Table.

During the turbulent days of the 16th century, a boatload of women from, it was said, Scandinavia, sought sanctuary here. They soon revealed themselves to be black witches who black-mailed others into feeding them by threatening curses. They were used to taking what they liked from market stalls without making any payments.

Goronwy ap Tudur was the only man in Anglesey brave enough to stand up to them. He had a third nipple himself, so he met the witches on equal terms and knew how to protect himself from witchcraft. One night, Bella Fawr (Big Bella), who was the chief witch, cast a spell on Goronwy's cattle. Goronwy happened to witness a large hare, which was Bella in animal form, sucking at one of his cows until it gave blood. He fired a silver bullet dusted with vervain at the hare, which limped back to Bella's cottage, where Goronwy found Bella sitting on a chair bleeding from both legs. Bella sought revenge by writing Goronwy's name on a scrap of parchment and throwing it into Wales' greatest cursing well, St. Eilian's near Menai bridge. This succeeded in piercing Goronwy's defences, but he stuck pins in a fungus called witches' butter and called Bella's name. This caused Bella so much pain that she eventually lifted the curse from Goronwy in exchange for Goronwy removing the pins.

Red Wharf Bay, Anglesey

The Walk

1. Face the Owain Glyndŵr Inn and go right, ignore the road forking right and go ahead as signposted for the beach (traeth). Reach Llys-y-Gwynt on your right and fork left down a 25% (1 in 4) gradient, towards Red Wharf Bay.

2. When the road bends left, turn right through a kissing gate along a signposted public footpath. Go ahead three paces and bear left downhill beside a hedge on your left. Turn left in the bottom corner and cross a ladder-stile. Turn right to cross a second ladder-stile. Go left down a track to pass between buildings and turn left, then right down a hedged path towards the sea.

3. Turn right along a track to walk with the sea on your left. Bear right to climb to a telephone box and turn left past St. Dona's Church on your left. Ignore a hedged track on your right, but bear left down a lane signposted as a public footpath.

4. Reach Ty-Llwyn on your right and fork right along a hedged track. Continue over stiles beside gates and enter the National Trust's Bryn Offa hillside, covered in gorse. Go ahead along the track for 250 yards and look for a concrete water-tank on your right. Bear right uphill to a stile in the top fence waymarked 'Llwybr yr Arfordir/Coastal Footpath'. Go ahead along the left-hand edge of a field adorned by gorse bushes.

5. Bear left over a waymarked ladder-stile and along the left-hand edge of a field. Bear left over a ladder-stile beside a gate in the corner ahead and walk with the hill fort associated with King Arthur's Round Table on your right. Turn sharply right at a track junction to head for a TV mast.

6. Go left along a road and pass a No Through Road to St. Iestyn's Church on your left. Go ahead 50 yards and turn right down a track signposted as a public footpath, with views of Snowdonia across the Menai Straits in front of you.

7. Turn left to pass the buildings of Tyn Llwyn on your right and take a gate ahead. Continue through a kissing gate beside the next gate ahead, turn right to pass the farmhouse on your right and turn left in the corner to walk down the right-hand edge of the field (towards Snowdonia). Take a kissing gate in the corner ahead to maintain your direction but with the hedge on your left in the next two fields. Go ahead along a hedged track to a road.

8. Go right along the road back to Llanddona and the Owain Glyndŵr Inn.

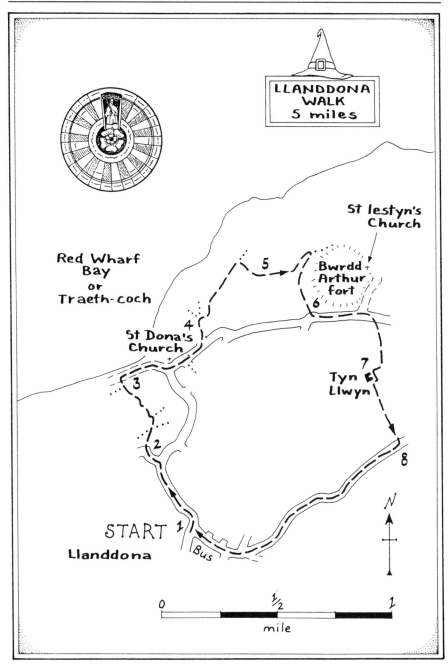

LLANDDONA
WALK
5 miles

St Iestyn's
Church

Red Wharf
Bay
or
Traeth-coch

5

Bwrdd
Arthur
fort

6

4

St Dona's
Church

3

Tyn
Llwyn

7

2

8

START

Llanddona

Bus

N

0   ½   1

mile

Denbigh Castle

2. Ɔenʀigh

Route: Denbigh — Gwaynynog — Dr. Johnson's Monument — Denbigh Castle — Denbigh.

Distance: 5 miles. Easy.

Map: OS Pathfinder 772 Denbigh.

Start: Lenten Pool, Denbigh, where the bus stops are and a signposted car park is close by (SJ 050661).

Access: Several bus services converge on Denbigh, including the no. 51 which comes from Rhyl, the nearest railway station. Telephone 01352 704035 for details.

The Dragon of Denbigh

Dragons are snakes that manage to drink the milk from a woman. This enables them to grow in size and sprout wings. The dragon may also symbolise the great energy pulsing through a place which needs to be tamed and used in a positive way. Denbigh was once notorious for its dragon and many people, let alone cattle and sheep, lost their lives to it. As St. George was unavailable, Sion Bodiau (Sir John of the Thumbs) came to the rescue. The fact that he had two thumbs on each hand indicated that he was equal to a dragon. The local women also promised him their favours should he succeed in ridding them of the beast, which had taken over the castle. Sion duly obliged, chopping off the dragon's head while it was counting his thumbs. The townspeople then lifted their hero onto their shoulders and paraded him around the town shouting 'Dim Bych!', meaning 'No Dragon!'. This was corrupted into Denbigh.

There is a very powerful dragon line, spirit path or ley slicing through Denbigh castle. Curiously, Robert Dudley, Earl of Leicester, the favourite of Queen Elizabeth I and, 'tis said in Clwyd, the father of her illegitimate son who was born at Plas Yn Eglwyseg, north of Llangollen (see walk no. 11 Valle Crucis Abbey), was brought up as Francis Bacon and was largely responsible for the plays ascribed to William Shakespeare, started to build a great new Protestant cathedral at Denbigh on this ley. It would have replaced the old cathedral at St. Asaph. A tiny cottage standing in the shadow of the castle walls on this line was the birthplace of one of the most interesting figures of the Victorian period. John

Rowlands, the illegitimate son of Elizabeth Parry and John Rowlands, suffered a harsh childhood, including eight years in St. Asaph workhouse. Crossing to the U.S.A. as a cabin boy, he met the benefactor, Henry Morton Stanley, whose name he was to adopt before famously uttering the words 'Dr. Livingstone, I presume?' in 1871. Dr. Samuel Johnson also came this way, staying with the local clergyman at Gwaynyog in 1774. A monument was erected near the Afon Ystrad to commemorate his visit.

The memorial to Dr Johnson

The Walk

1. With the Hand Inn to your right, go ahead along Llys y Grawys. Turn left up Glas Meadows Lane. This narrows to a footpath before meeting a road. Go right for 20 yards and turn left up Ystad Llewelyn. When this road bends left, turn right along an enclosed and signposted public footpath. Emerge over a stile onto a field.

2. Go down the left-hand side of this field, then bear right diagonally across the next. Go right up a track to Galch Hill, cross a stile and continue along the right-hand edge of this and the next field. Ignore a stile in the fence on your right in the second field, take a gate ahead and bear slightly left across the third field. Continue through a gate in the fence ahead and along a track in the middle of the field.

3. Go ahead across the drive of Gwaynynog, the house on your left. Take a track to a stile beside a gate, cross it and follow the left-hand edge of pasture to continue over another stile beside a gate in the next corner. Bear left, as waymarked, go ahead over a stone stile to the left of a gate and cut across the neck of a field. Cross a stile to the right of a gate in the hedge ahead. Bear right to walk with woodland on your right.

4. Turn right over a stile beside a gate and immediately turn left to descend with a belt of trees on your left. Continue over a stile in a corner to go down a woodland path. Reach a stile in the bottom fence but don't cross it yet! Divert right through the wood to emerge over a stile and bear left down towards the river to see the monument to Dr. Samuel Johnson.

5. Retrace your steps to the woodland path and return to the stile in its bottom fence. Cross it to bear left through a meadow.

Keep with this path as it passes through forest and between hedgerows to reach a road.

6. Turn right and ignore a stile in the hedge on your left after about 100 yards. Continue for another 100 yards and turn left into a drive and immediately turn left over a stile, then turn right, as waymarked. Follow this meadow path, keeping above the river on your right and going ahead through two field gates. Continue through a small gate to enter woodland and go ahead along a narrow path when the woodland track descends towards the river. Follow a lane until it bends left, then go straight ahead with a hedged track to reach a road.

7. Turn left up the road and bear right at the sign for Denbigh Castle. With the castle entrance on your right, go ahead towards St. Hilary's Tower, passing the birthplace of Henry Morton Stanley (born John Rowlands in the pink cottage to your right). Bear left to go through the late 13th century Burgess Gate, descend steps and turn right along Highgate. Turn sharply left down Portland Place to return to Lenten Pool.

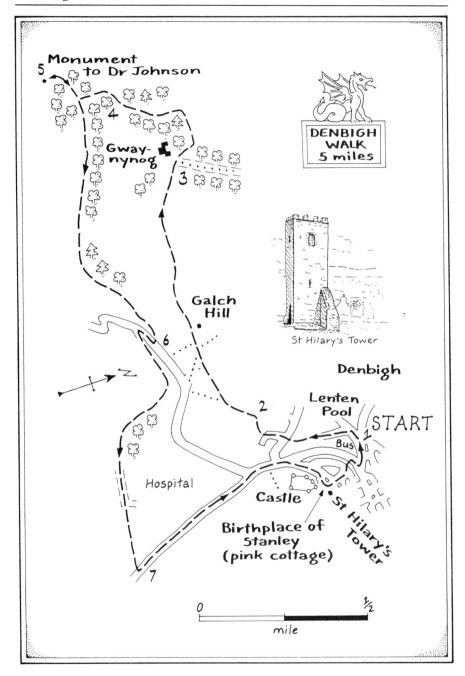

Monument to Dr Johnson

5

4

Gway-nynog

3

Galch Hill

6

DENBIGH WALK 5 miles

St Hilary's Tower

Denbigh

Lenten Pool

START

2

Bus

1

Hospital

Castle

St Hilary's Tower

Birthplace of Stanley (pink cottage)

7

0   ½
mile

3. holywell

Route: Holywell – St. Winifred's Well – Basingwerk Abbey – Holywell.

Distance: 3 miles. Easy.

Map: OS Pathfinder 755 Holywell.

Start: Bus station in Holywell, near which is a car park.

Access: Holywell is served by buses from all directions. Telephone 01352 704035 for details.

St. Winifred's Well

Of all the holy wells in Wales, this is the most famous. It was the terminus of the pilgrimage route from St. David's, crossing Wales diagonally, while English monarchs such as Richard I (in 1189) came here. The well acquired a reputation for miraculous cures. None were as remarkable as the event that caused the healing well to rise up. Winifred, or Gwenfrewi, was the niece of St. Beuno and acknowledged to be extremely beautiful. One day she stayed at home while her parents went to hear Beuno preach. A local chieftain called Caradog took the opportunity to visit her and ask her to be his mistress. She demurred by saying she wasn't worthy of such a noble as he, excused herself to prepare in her chamber and made her escape from it. Caradog pursued and caught her and cut off her head. Some accounts have the severed head rolling downhill to where the well is now. Beuno, who was descended from a cousin of the Virgin Mary (whose mother was the British St. Anne, taken to the Holy Land by Joseph of Arimathea to marry his brother), cursed Caradog and caused the ground to swallow him up. His descendants (indicating that Caradog was already married when he took a fancy to Gwenfrewi) were made to bark like dogs until they sought penance. The saint then resuscitated Gwenfrewi by placing the head back on her body and the two were miraculously joined again. A white scar remained around her neck as a reminder of what had happened. Previously called Breuy, the maiden was now called Guenn (white) Vreuy. The healing well rose up where her head or her blood had fallen. This valley, now boasting lakes, had previously been dry and was called Sychnant (dry vale).

St Winifred's Well

The Walk

1. With your back to the Hotel Victoria, go left along the pedestrianised High Street. Turn right at its end, cross a road, go ahead down steps and down Well Street. Pass Plas Dewi on your left and continue down a path to the holy well, with an Anglican church above it to your right and a Roman Catholic chapel directly above the well to your left. Go left to the road and turn right down its pavement to reach the entrance to the well, on your right.

2. Continue along the pavement until the Royal Oak Inn is reached on your right. Turn right here and immediately left to follow a path which soon passes a lake on your right. Turn right at the head of this lake to pass above the Battery Works on your left and climb past a chimney ahead into woodland. Turn left along the course of a dismantled railway. Pass above a lake on your left before taking the second fork on your left down to its shore.

3. Walk with the lake on your left and continue past the Victoria Mill and the Abbey Wire Mill on your left. Go ahead to the Abbey Farm Museum and Visitor Centre. Bear right to pass the ruins of Basingwerk Abbey on your left. Look for steps rising on your right.

4. Turn right up the steps and turn right along the course of the dismantled railway. Follow this all the way past three lakes on your right and fork right, as signposted, for St. Winefride's Halt. Bear right to reach the road and turn left to retrace your steps to the start, soon passing the well again on your left.

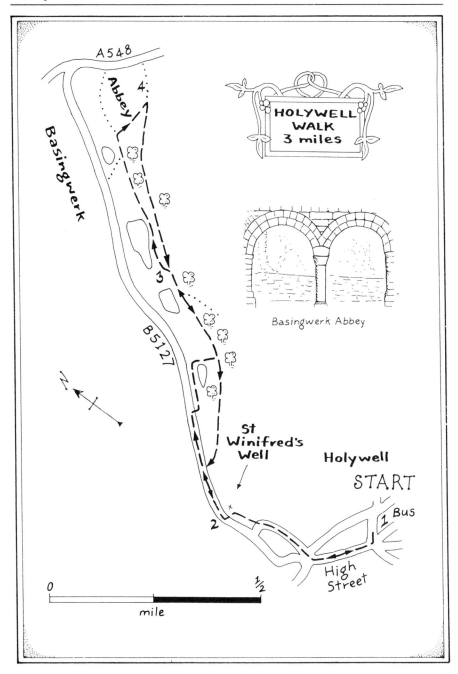

Basingwerk Abbey

4. nant gwrtheyrn

Route: Llithfaen – Nant Gwrtheyrn – Porth-y-nant – Ciliau Isaf – Llithfaen.

Distance: 4 miles. Moderate.

Map: O.S. Pathfinder 801 Llanaelhaearn.

Start: Crossroads and bus stop in Llithfaen (SH 356432).

Access: Llithfaen is on the B4417 three miles west of its junction with the A499 at Llanaelhaearn. It is served by bus no. 27 from Pwllheli (the nearest railway station). Telephone 01286 679535 for times.

Vortigern's Valley

That archtraitor Vortigern, the usurper who invited Hengist and Horsa into what was to become England, fled here after the 'Treachery of the Long Knives' had turned the country against him and swung support behind Ambrosius Aurelianus. He didn't last long, with one account claiming that he was struck by lightning as divine punishment. It does seem that he escaped, finding further refuge at Little Doward Hill in the Wye Valley and, finally, in Brittany. This was probably in 465 AD. This valley couldn't escape from its curse, however. Monks from Clynnog-fawr had cursed the place after failing to convert its pagan inhabitants. They decreed that no two lovers from Nant Gwrtheyrn would ever marry, that none of the inhabitants would be buried in consecrated ground and that the village would die. The village did indeed die, although there was a brief revival in the mid-19th century when the quarries were working. Now there is another revival, with the Welsh National Language Centre occupying the forsaken quarry village. If you would like to come here and learn Welsh, telephone 0175 885334, or write to Canolfan Iaith Genedlaethol Nant Gwrtheyrn, Llithfaen, Pwllheli, Gwynedd, LL53 6PA.

Two young people here did decide to defy the ban on their marrying. Their names were Rhys and Meinir. According to custom, Meinir pretended to play hard to get and hid in a hollow tree before her wedding. Rhys and the other men of the village couldn't find her, while Meinir found herself unable to escape from the tree. The wedding couldn't take place and Rhys was driven to insanity. Later the hollow tree was struck by lightning and the skeleton of Meinir was revealed. When Rhys heard the news he died of a broken heart and the two lovers were placed in the same coffin. When the horse pulling the cart with their coffin to be buried at the church in Clynnog came to the steep climb out of the valley, the cart ran away and plunged over the cliff into the sea, giving the lovers a watery grave.

The remains of Porth-y-Nant quarry

The Walk

1. Face the village shop and turn right, then right again to take a lane which climbs to a forestry plantation. Walk down a ravine with trees on your right for 250 yards.

2. Turn right down a track into the forest. Bear right with this track, then left downhill to return to the road. Go right down the road to the Welsh National Language Centre at Nant Gwrtheyrn, passing its car park on your right.

3. Follow the waymarked path down to the beach. Pass the remains of Porth-y-Nant Quarry on your left and reach waymark post no. 6.

4. Climb steps to take the waymarked path uphill to a higher path, which you turn right along to walk above the sea on your right. Go ahead through a gap in a wall into Gallt y Bwlch Site of Special Scientific Interest, with its stunted sessile oaks. Continue towards Ciliau Isaf, turning left up steps to a small metal gate just before you reach this farmhouse.

5. Go ahead along the farm track, as waymarked. Cross two cattle grids and ignore paths leading left as you continue to the B4417 road.

6. Turn left along the B4417 road to return to the bus stop at the crossroads in Llithfaen.

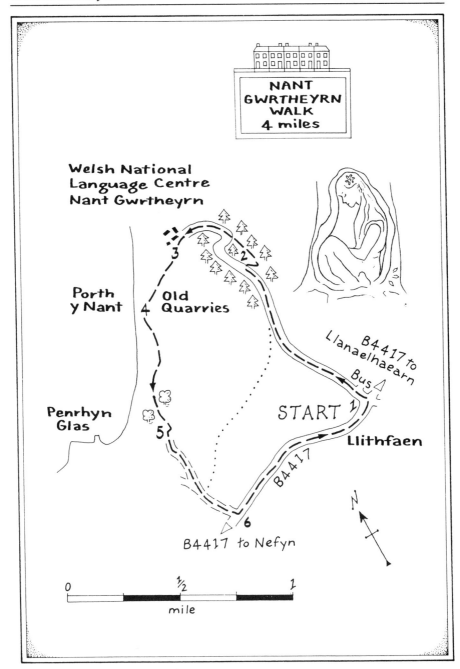

NANT
GWRTHEYRN
WALK
4 miles

Welsh National
Language Centre
Nant Gwrtheyrn

Porth
y Nant

Old
Quarries

Penrhyn
Glas

START

Llithfaen

B4417 to
Llanaelhaearn

Bus

B4417

B4417 to Nefyn

N

0   ½   1
mile

The Nant Gwrtheyrn walk: a waymarked path leads down to the beach

5. gartb dorwen

Route: Inigo Jones Slate Works – Llain-ffynnan – Garth Uchaf – Uwchlaw'r-rhos – Tyddyn Bach – Penygroes – Lon Eifion – Inigo Jones Slate Works.

Distance: 3½ miles. Easy.

Map: O.S. Pathfinder 785 Penygroes.

Start: Inigo Jones Slate Works (SH 471552).

Access: The start is beside the A487 one mile north of Penygroes and six miles south of Caernarfon. Buses nos. 1 (Blaenau Ffestiniog – Caernarfon) and 2 (Dolgellau – Caernarfon) stop by request at Inigo Jones Slate Works.

Garth Dorwen

This farm is the setting for a famous fairy story. Long ago an old man lived here with his wife. They hired a servant girl called Eilian at Caernarfon Fair. She would spend the long winter evenings spinning in the meadow by the light of the moon, when the fairies came out to sing and dance near her. One day in the spring Eilian ran off with them.

The old woman at Garth Dorwen was the local midwife. Some time after Eilian's disappearance a man called on the night of a full moon to take the midwife on his horse's back to his wife at Rhos-y-Cowrt. When they reached an old fort in the centre of the moor, known as Bryn y Pibion, they entered to find a room which the old woman was to describe as the finest she had seen in her life. In it lay the wife in bed.

After the baby was born, the man gave the midwife some ointment and told her to anoint the baby's eyes with it, but not to get any on her own. One of her eyes itched, however, and the midwife accidentally rubbed some of the ointment on it. The fine room was changed into a cave, the bed was turned into stones and withered bracken, while the wife became the lost servant, Eilian.

Some time afterwards, whilst at Caernarfon market, the old woman saw the husband and asked him how Eilian was. The man replied that she was well, then asked with which eye the old woman could see him. She pointed to the one which she had rubbed with the ointment. The man immediately put it out with a bullrush, thus depriving her of this special sight.

Looking west from the track near Garth Uchaf

The Walk

1. Cross the A487 from Inigo Jones Slate Works and take the signposted track, soon going through a gate. Walk with a stream on your right-hand side. Pass buildings on your left, go ahead through a gate and keep to the slightly raised path which goes over a small slate slab footbridge and keeps near the hedge on your left. Go ahead through a small gate squeezed between a wall on your left and a stream on your right. Continue along a narrow, enclosed, path and emerge through a kissing gate to bear right beside a fence to pass through another small gate and a house on your right.

2. Reach a lane (Ty'n Weirgoldd) and turn right, past the houses on your left, then turn left past the last house. Go through a kissing gate into a field and cross it to an old stone stile in the right-hand corner. Continue beside a wall on your right in the next field until a corner where a gate invites you to turn right. Go through it to follow a track past a house on your left, then past the buildings of Garth Uchaf on your left.

3. Turn left at a T-junction with a lane and follow it towards Uwchlaw'r-rhos. As you approach these buildings, turn sharply right along an enclosed track which opens out and where the path continues over a ladder stile in the fence ahead.

4. Cross the next field, full of gorse bushes, to a small gate in a corner ahead on your right, with a plantation of conifer trees behind the wall on your right. Go ahead along an enclosed path to emerge below the house of Tyddyn Bach. Walk with the forest's perimeter wall on your right, then bear left with a high fence on your left to join Tyddyn Bach's access track. Go right along it to the A487.

5. Turn left along the A487 into Penygroes. Turn right along a track opposite a bus stop. Continue along the right-hand edges of three fields.

6. Turn right along the Lon Eifion Cycle Path, formerly a railway, back to the Inigo Jones Slate Works on your right.

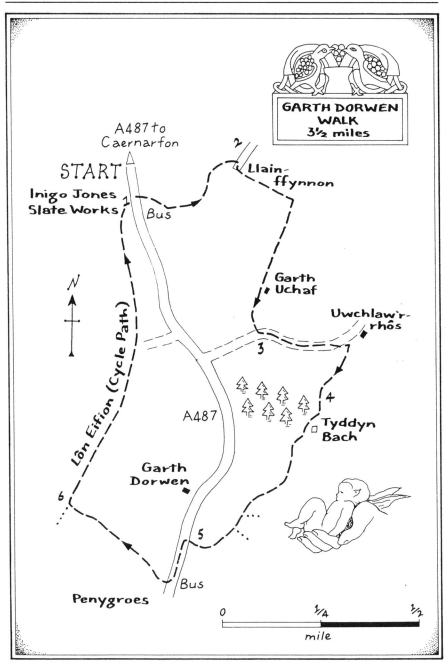

GARTH DORWEN
WALK
3½ miles

A487 to
Caernarfon

START

Inigo Jones
Slate Works

Bus

Llain-
ffynnon

Garth
Uchaf

Uwchlaw'r-
rhôs

N

Lôn Eifion (Cycle Path)

A487

Tyddyn
Bach

Garth
Dorwen

Penygroes

Bus

0   ¼   ½
mile

6. cricciech

Route: Llanystumdwy — David Lloyd George Memorial — Dwyfor Valley — Criccieth — Ynysgain — Llanystumdwy.

Distance: 6 miles. Easy.

Maps: O.S. Pathfinder 822 Pwllheli and Outdoor Leisure 18 Harlech & Bala areas.

Start: David Lloyd George Museum, Llanystumdwy (SH 477384).

Access: Llanystumdwy is just north of the A497 two miles west of Criccieth, where there is a station on the Cambrian Coast Line. Bus no. 3 links it with Pwllheli, Porthmadog and Blaenau Ffestiniog.

Criccieth

Criccieth Castle stands on a rocky promontory overlooking Cardigan Bay. CADW have produced an excellent guide to the castle, which was built by the Welsh in the time of Llywelyn Fawr, in the early 13th century. It fell to the English in 1283. Its position demands the attention of ley hunters as a major ley or spirit path would appear to go through it, coming from the west. Cutting across the tip of Pen-ychain at SH 436352, this ley passes Llanbedrog's church at SH 329315 and an old fort at SH 322314, then another old fort at SH 230283 (near Rhiw) to reach the old church on the sands at Aberdaron, dedicated to St. Hynwyn, a nephew of King Arthur. This was where pilgrims assembled before going to Bardsey Island. Extend the line and it comes to an interesting stone on Trwyn Maen Melyn (yellowstone point) at SH 139252. This stone, which is covered by yellow moss, actually points out the line of this ley as it goes westwards into the sea, north of the mystical isle of Bardsey. Bardsey is said to be where 20,000 saints lie buried. Like Iona, it is a repository for the bodies of the great and good, including Myrddin (Merlin). It was probably the island to which the grievously wounded King Arthur was taken after Camlan. Spirit paths or leys converge on the tips of peninsulas and the offshore island, in this case Bardsey off the tip of the Lleyn Peninsula, is where the favoured dead souls go. There seem to be two points for leys to aim at here. One is Mynydd Anelog at SH 152272, whose name actually suggests 'aiming' and whose peak is a landmark. Perhaps 'male' energy lines went here? The other is the old church dedicated to St. Mary (for 'female' energy lines?), near the pointing rock at Trwyn Maen Melyn and above the holy well, also dedicated to St. Mary, from which some pilgrims took their final drink before risking the crossing to Bardsey.

Criccieth's name is said to be derived from a cry of distress from the inhabitants of the drowned land of Cantre'r Gwaelod. This fertile land stretched from Bardsey to St. David's, where we now have Cardigan Bay. Chronicles assure us that this land was drowned when Seithenyn the Drunkard neglected the sea walls and allowed the water to break through one stormy night. The characters in the story fit the sixth century AD, when some flooding must have taken place. Scientists agree that land now under the waters of Cardigan Bay was drowned, but as long ago as 3500 BC. Perhaps folk memories are much longer than we think. Great storms and floods still take place along this coast, while earthquakes have been recorded, as in July, 1984. A sudden and catastrophic sea on the night of 28th October, 1927 destroyed the Tramway which ran between Pwllheli and Llanbedrog.

The valley of the Afon Dwyfor is full of peaceful glades where, no doubt, fairies can be seen. It seems an appropriate spot for the memorial and grave of the famous statesman David Lloyd George. Born in Manchester, he was brought up in Llanystumdwy, where there is a museum devoted to him.

The path up the valley of the Afon Dwyfor

The Walk

1. *Go right to approach the bridge over the Afon Dwyfor. Turn right immediately before it, along a minor road. After about 100 yards, bear left down a signposted public footpath, passing below David Lloyd George's grave and memorial.*

2. Follow the riverside path, going upstream with the Afon Dwyfor on your left and passing through delightful woodland. This clear path eventually reaches a stone wall. Bear right through an arch in it to emerge on a lane.

3. Turn left along this lane to a junction with the B4411 road. Turn right along this road, towards Criccieth.

4. Turn right along a track signposted as a public footpath. Reach a small wood and fork left through it to leave by a kissing gate at its far end. Continue along the left-hand edge of a field. Turn left when you reach another kissing gate to go through it and turn right immediately to walk along the right-hand edge of the next field.

5. Go through a kissing gate and bear left along a path marked by slate slabs diagonally across a meadow to reach the B4411 road. Go right along this road to come to a housing estate on your right.

6. Take a metal kissing gate on your right to walk along the pavement of the housing estate, with the houses on your right. Approach a children's playground and turn right, then turn left along a passageway. Go right along a lane to pass Bryn Awelon on your left. This was once the home of David Lloyd George.

7. Bear left at a fork down the narrow lane towards the sea. Cross

the A497 carefully, then a bridge over the railway and continue to the seafront. Go left to walk with the sea on your right and Criccieth Castle ahead. Follow the road around to the castle's entrance.

8. Retrace your steps along the seafront, with the sea now on your left, to the western edge of Criccieth. Follow the coastal path to the National Trust site of Ynysgain. Continue with the sea on your left to reach the mouth of the Afon Dwyfor. Bear right upstream, with the river on your left.

9. Turn right through a gate to follow a lane away from the river. Turn left, inland, with this and cross a bridge over the railway to reach the A497 road. Cross this carefully and turn left along its verge. Bear right at a fork to return to Llanystumdwy.

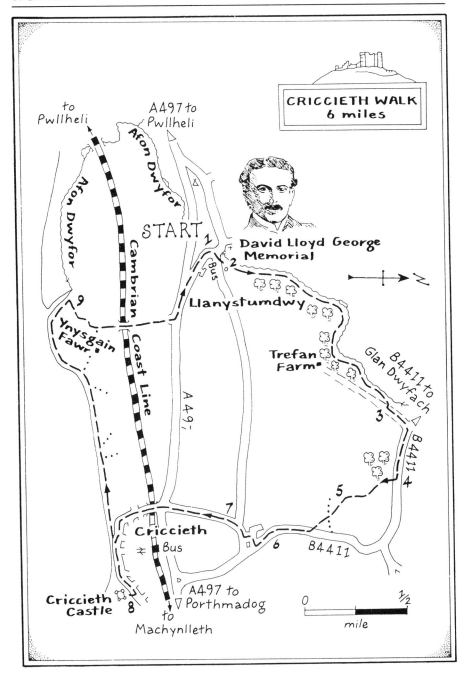

7. Beddgelert

Route: Beddgelert – Gelert's Grave – Mynydd Sygyn – Sygun Copper Mine – Beddgelert.

Distance: 3½ miles. Strenuous.

Map: O.S. Outdoor Leisure 17 Snowdonia – Snowdon area.

Start: The bus stop in Beddgelert, near which is a car park (SH 588481).

Access: Beddgelert is at the junction of the A498 with the A4085. Bus no. 11 connects Beddgelert with Llanberis and Caernarfon, while bus no. 97 comes from Porthmadog (the nearest railway station).

Beddgelert

Gelert was the favourite greyhound of Prince Llywelyn but one morning it did not answer the call to join in the chase. The prince went without him and had a disappointing day. When he returned, he found Gelert coming to greet him. Llywelyn was startled to see that the dog was dripping with blood. The suspicious prince thought that Gelert might have attacked his two year old son and, indeed, when he inspected his son's bedchamber, the cradle was overturned, the child seemed to be missing and there was blood everywhere. Jumping to the conclusion that Gelert had attacked his son, he plunged his sword into the greyhound, killing it. Then a cry was heard from beneath the overturned cradle. The boy was alive and well, whilst nearby was the torn body of a wolf. Llywelyn realised too late that his faithful hound had saved his son's life by protecting him from the wolf. Repenting his rashness, he buried Gelert under this noble tomb and made sure that the story is known to this day. The village's name even means 'Gelert's Grave'.

Above Sygun Copper Mine, with Dinas Emrys across the valley

Across the valley from Sygun Copper Mine, at the top of the wooded hill, is Dinas Emrys. This is where Vortigern fled to after his erstwhile allies the Saxons had turned against the Britons. He was advised to build a secure castle here but the builders found whatever they constructed fell down. It was determined to hold a foundation ceremony and sprinkle the ground with the blood of a boy born without a father, having, of course, put the boy to death. When the child was found, he dared to ask Vortigern why he was to be sacrificed. When told it was so that his citadel should stand, the boy dared the king's advisers to reveal what was under the proposed site. When they couldn't say, he told them there was a pool, which they soon confirmed by digging. He then asked them what was in the pool and once again had to inform them. The child revealed two vases, containing a tent. The assembled company marvelled as the young Myrddin (Merlin – for it was he, the famous magician of the future King Arthur) correctly predicted that the unfolded tent would reveal two sleeping drag-

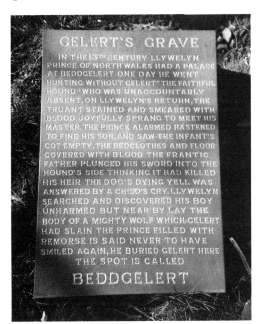

Gelert's grave

ons, one white and one red. These awoke to fight each other. At first the white one seemed to be winning, but the red dragon finally triumphed. Myrddin interpreted this as meaning that the red dragon of the Britons would eventually over-come the white dragon of the Saxons. He then or-dered Vortigern to depart from this spot (he went to Nant Gwrtheyrn), which was called Dinas Emrys, the citadel of Emrys, after the young magician, Myrddin Emrys.

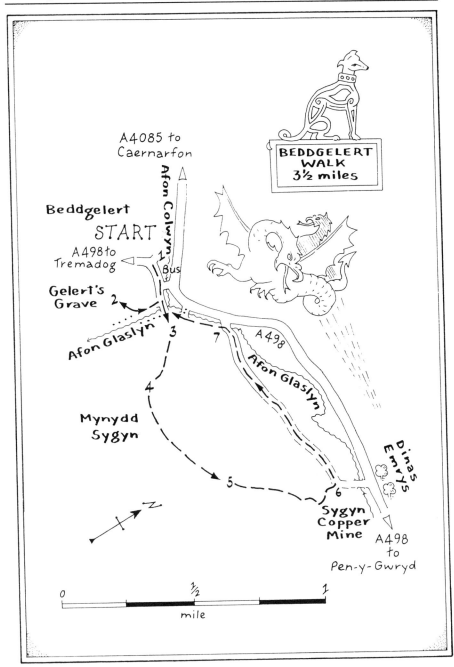

A4085 to
Caernarfon

BEDDGELERT
WALK
3½ miles

Beddgelert
START
A498 to
Tremadog

Afon Colwyn

Bus

Gelert's
Grave
2

Afon Glaslyn
3   7   A498

4

Mynydd
Sygyn   Afon Glaslyn

5   6

Dinas
Emrys

Sygyn
Copper
Mine   A498
to
Pen-y-Gwryd

N

0   ½   1
                    mile

The Walk

1. Walk into the centre of Beddgelert but when the road turns left across a bridge go straight ahead along a lane with the river on your left. Approach a footbridge across the Afon Glaslyn near its confluence with the Afon Colwyn but don't cross it yet. Turn right through a small metal gate just before it and follow the path to Gelert's Grave. After walking 300 yards beside the Afon Glaslyn on your left, turn right, as waymarked, to the grave.

2. Retrace your steps from Gelert's Grave to the footbridge and this time turn right to cross it. Ignore paths bearing left and right beside the river. Go straight ahead past the end of a row of cottages on your left, turn left for 50 yards, then turn right, as signposted up a shaded lane. Continue through a small gate and climb with a steep path, sometimes scrambling up the hillside.

3. Fork left and pass through a gap in a wall. Soon turn right up a waymarked path which climbs to a small gate in a wall.

4. Go through the gate and bear left to reach a cairn on top of a ridge.

5. Descend with a path on your left down to Sygun Copper Mine.

6. Turn left along a track which soon becomes a lane, with the Afon Glaslyn away to your right. Approach a bridge over the river.

7. Just before the bridge, turn left over a ladder stile to follow a path past rhododendron bushes and past the river on your right. Go ahead to reach the footbridge crossed on the outward journey. Return over it to retrace your steps into Beddgelert.

8. Llyn tegíd (Bala Lake)

Route: Bala Tourist Information Centre – Llanycil Picnic Site – Penlan – Llanycil Picnic Site – Bala Tourist Information Centre.

Distance: 2½ miles. Moderate.

Map: Either OS Pathfinder 825 Bala or OS Outdoor Leisure 18 Snowdonia – Harlech & Bala areas.

Start: Bala Tourist Information Centre (SH 922356).

Access: Bala is served by bus no. 94 from Barmouth, Dolgellau and Wrexham. Telephone 01286 679535 for times.

Llyn Tegid (Bala Lake)

Llyn Tegid is the largest natural lake in Wales, but it wasn't always four and a half miles long by half a mile wide. Once upon a time an evil king had his palace where water now covers the land. His name was Tegid Foel and his wife was none other than Ceridwen, the hag aspect of the Earth Goddess with the inspirational and rejuvenating cauldron that became known as the Holy Grail. It was from this that the three drops were accidentally swallowed by Gwion Bach, the son of the blacksmith of Llanfair Caereinion, but that is another story.

The evil Tegid Foel believed himself to be above natural law, but if he listened he would hear the words 'vengeance will come' carried by the wind. One night it did come, while a great banquet was taking place to celebrate the birth of a first child to his son's wife. A harpist was engaged to entertain the gathering and he took note of the warning of impending vengeance whilst the guests guzzled food and drink. The harpist followed a small bird out of the palace, leaving his harp behind. The bird led him up the side of the valley until he fell asleep from exhaustion. He awoke to discover a lake at his feet. His harp floated to him on the surface of the water. This was the origin of Llyn Tegid. Another story tells of an overflowing well at Llangywer causing the appearance of the lake, while there is a prediction that the modern town of Bala will be drowned one day, with the waters extending to Llanfor. In the 18th century, another harpist, called Charles, was known to offer Communion bread to the dogs at Llanycil, showing that he had sold his soul to the devil. One evening he drowned in the lake and a puff of smoke marked the spot.

Llyn Tegid boasts its own version of a Loch Ness Monster. It is seen regularly, with fishermen being startled by it at dawn in the spring of 1995. Old Christmas Eve (4th January) is the time to see strange lights in the sky above the lake, which marks a major fault line. King Arthur was brought up at Caer Gai, between Llanycil and Llanuwchllyn, with his foster-brother Sir Kay (the Cai from whom this old Roman fort is named).

Overlooking Llyn Tegid

The Walk

1. Face the lake and go right, keeping the lake on your left. There is a pavement beside the A494, but if conditions are alright, it is also possible to follow a path below the road, screened by trees and near the shore of the lake. In any case, go left to walk with the lake on your left and reach the car park and picnic site at Llanycil, where you continue along the pavement of the A494 (having climbed up to it at the picnic site if taking the path below the road) for 250 yards. The church at Llanycil is ahead but you don't go as far as it.

2. Look for three tracks converging on the A494, across this road on your right. The left-hand track is the access lane for Abercelyn, where ramblers are very welcome to stay for bed and breakfast (tel. 01678 521109). Turn right to cross the A494 carefully and take the middle of these three tracks, crossing a cattle grid and going uphill. Walk up a firm track with a fence on your left. The waymarked bridleway which forks right is the route by which you will descend on the return half of this walk. When the firm track curves round to the right, keep ahead, near the hedge on your left and soon passing the edge of delightful natural deciduous woodland on your right. Continue over a waymarked stile, through woodland and across another waymarked stile. Walk with woodland on your right to reach a ruin on your right.

3. Bear right to a primitive stile marked by a yellow arrow in the top right-hand corner of this field. Cross it and go ahead along the left-hand edge of this high pasture. Go ahead through a waymarked gate and approach the farm of Penlan. Turn left through a gate in the corner but don't proceed towards the farm buildings.

4. Turn right and right again to take another gate and walk away from Penlan along a hedged public bridleway, descending towards Bala Lake. Continue, as waymarked by blue arrows, taking a gate at the end of the hedged track and in the far side of the field after it. The right of way keeps near the right-hand edge of the next pasture as it descends towards the lake. A muddy surface and the intrusion of gorse bushes has led to a popular path going above these bushes and affording fine views over the lake before descending to the line of the right of way on your right.

5. Pass a house on your right as you descend with the track, still with a fence on right and a wooded slope on your left. Go ahead through a gate to descend now with a fence on your left. Rejoin your outward track and go left down it to retrace your steps back to the road and the Tourist Information Centre in Bala, this time keeping the lake on your right.

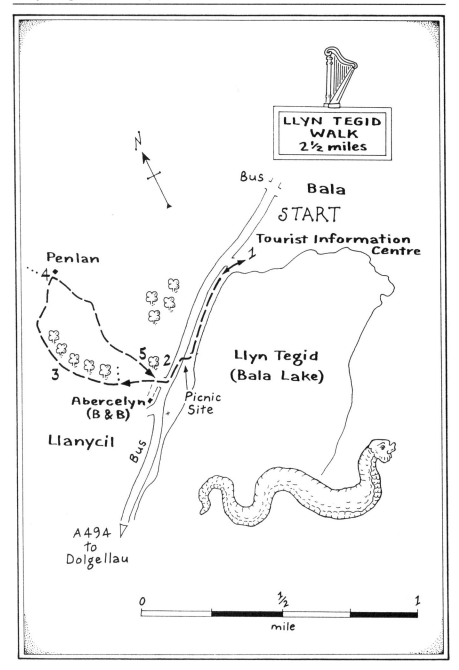

LLYN TEGID
WALK
2 ½ miles

N

Bus

Bala

START

Tourist Information
Centre

Penlan

4

Llyn Tegid
(Bala Lake)

5 2

3

Abercelyn
(B & B)

Picnic
Site

Llanycil

Bus

A494
to
Dolgellau

0   ½   1

mile

9. Llanꝺꝺerꝼel

Route: Llandderfel – Llyn Bodweni – Bryn-Banon – Ty'n-y-bwlch – Llandderfel.

Distance: 4½ miles. Moderate.

Map: OS Pathfinder 825 Bala.

Start: St. Derfel's Church, Llandderfel (SH 982371).

Access: Llandderfel is served by bus no. 94 from Barmouth, Dolgellau, Bala and Wrexham. Telephone 01286 679535 for times).

St. Derfel Gadarn (the Mighty)

Derfel was the son of Riwal Mawr, the son of Emyr Llydaw and the brother of Amwn Ddu, making him the cousin of St. Tydecho (see walk no. 13 Dinas Mawddwy). Derfel earned the epithet Gadarn ('the Mighty') because of his deeds as a warrior. He was one of King Arthur's knights and distinguished himself at the Battle of Camlan. He was also famous for having descended into the Underworld and having found his way back, rescuing others from the Underworld at the same time. This tradition led to hundreds of people gathering at his church on his saint's day, 5th April, to worship his effigy in the hope that St. Derfel would deliver them out of hell. The wooden effigy was of Derfel mounted on a horse and holding a staff. Remnants of the wooden horse and staff survive in the church. Come the Reformation and Thomas Cromwell had the effigy of Derfel sent to London, despite the local people raising the immense sum of £40 as a bribe for his agent.

At Smithfield Market on 22nd May, 1538, St. Derfel's effigy fulfilled a prophecy by setting fire to a forest. It was used in the bonfire for the burning of a Franciscan Observant friar whose name was Forest. The friar had denied King Henry VIII's right to call himself the supreme head of the Church of England.

Looking back up the Dee Valley from the return path to Llandderfel

The Walk

1. Face St. Derfel's Church and go right, out of the village and soon passing Maes y Priordy on your left. Turn left through a gate next to a public footpath signpost and follow a grassy track which is enclosed at first, then overlooks a cemetery on your left and has a hedge on your right. Bear left and climb with the track which affords views across the valley on your left and has gorse bushes forming the hedge on your right.

2. Continue through a waymarked gate to walk with a forest on your right and a fence on your left. The Berwyn hills can be seen across the valley of the Dee on your left. Go ahead along a woodland track when the fence on your left bears left. The fence returns to your left and you come to a fork. Do not bear left near the fence. Do bear right, uphill, through the woodland, as waymarked by a yellow arrow. Fork left, downhill, at a junction of four paths. Climb to another junction and bear right, uphill, as waymarked by a yellow arrow. Soon ignore a path which descends from the right to join yours. Go ahead through the forest to emerge over a stile in the corner of pasture and go ahead, as waymarked, with the forest behind a fence on your right. Pass a lake (Llyn Bodweni) on your left. Go ahead over a stile, past rhododendron bushes, past the tip of a lake and a cattle grid on your left, straight across a firm track and take a stile to the right of a waymarked gate ahead. Follow the track past trees on your left and rhododendron bushes on your right. Bear left to cross a stream then fork right to descend to a track.

3. Bear slightly left to cross the track and go over a stile. Take the waymarked path downhill on your right. Cross pasture and go through a patch of woodland, descend to a gate in the corner of a field and take it to follow the fieldpath down to a road, which

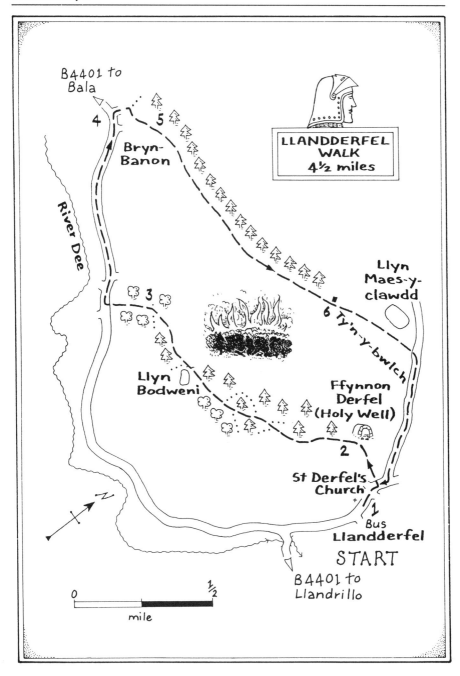

B4401 to
Bala

4 5

Bryn-
Banon

**LLANDDERFEL
WALK
4½ miles**

River Dee

3

Llyn
Maes-y-
clawdd

6 Ty'n-y-bwlch

Llyn
Bodweni

Ffynnon
Derfel
(Holy Well)

2

St Derfel's
Church

1

Bus
Llandderfel

START

B4401 to
Llandrillo

N

0   ½
mile

is gained by a gate next to a public footpath signpost. Go right along the road. Arenig Fawr's 2800 ft summit can be seen to the left ahead. Pass the entrance for Bryn-Banon on your right.

4. Turn right along the signposted public footpath which serves as another entrance for Bryn-Banon on your right. Follow the main track to a farm and bear right to pass it on your left, taking a waymarked gate.

5. Continue with an afforested slope on your left and a view over pasture on your right. The right of way follows a wall on your left, just below the perimeter fence on the forest. Look backwards to gain a view up the valley of the Dee to Bala lake. As the forest on your left comes to an end, take a lower path, as waymarked, to take a walled path to come to a waymarked bar-stile. Continue along the right-hand edge of pasture.

6. Continue through a gate in the corner and pass below Ty'n-y-bwlch. Follow its access track past the lake Llyn Maes-y-clawdd on your left. Reach a lane and turn right down it back to Llandderfel, keeping right at a junction.

10. llangar

Route: Cynwyd – River Dee – All Saints' Church – Cynwyd.

Distance: 2 ¼ miles. Easy.

Map: OS Pathfinder 805 Corwen.

Start: Bus shelter, Cynwyd (SJ 057412).

Access: Cynwyd is served by bus no. 94 from Wrexham, Dolgellau and Barmouth. Telephone 01352 704035 for details.

All Saints' Church, Llangar

This ancient church represents many that had their sites chosen for supernatural reasons. It was intended to be built at Cynwyd but the masons found that the stones kept being mysteriously removed overnight. A wise man finally advised them that God mustn't want the church to be built there and said that they should hunt a white stag. Where they raised the white stag would be the place to build the church. So the white stag was raised at the spot where All Saints' Church now stands. The original name for the parish wasn't Llangar but Llan-garw-gwyn, meaning 'the church of the white stag'. The white stag no doubt stood for purity. An old rhyme went:

'It was raised at Llangar;
It was killed at Moel Lladdfa;
It was buried at Fronguddio;
It decayed at Y Bedren.'

The Walk

1. With your back to Cynwyd bus shelter, go left along the pavement of the B4401 road to pass St. John's Church (built in 1855) on your left. Turn left down a signposted public footpath, which is enclosed by hedges. Emerge in the corner of a field and go ahead along the left-hand edge of this and the next two fields. Cross the course of a dismantled railway to reach the River Dee.

2. Bear right to walk downstream with the river on your left. Pass an old footbridge on your left. Cut across the old railway line again and take the track ahead until it bends right. Turn left through a gate to visit the old church of All Saints', Llangar.

All Saints' church, Llangar

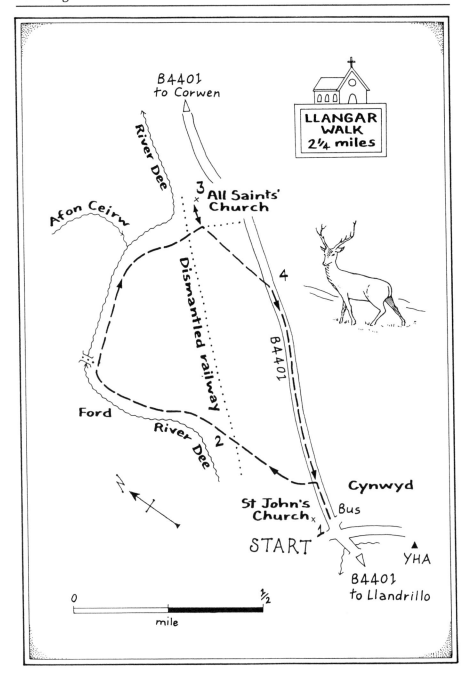

3. Return through the gate and go left to resume the track, soon bearing right. Approach farm buildings and go ahead as the track bends left, taking a gate and crossing the top of a kitchen garden. Continue along a hedged path and eventually emerge on the B4401 road.

4. Turn right to walk along the road back to Cynwyd.

11. valle crucis abbey

Route: Llangollen – Valle Crucis Abbey – Castell Dinas Bran.

Distance: 6½ miles. Strenuous (unless the climb up Castell Dinas Bran is omitted, making this an easy walk).

Maps: OS Pathfinders 805 Corwen and 806 Llangollen & Wrexham South.

Start: Tourist Information Centre, Llangollen (SJ 215420).

Access: Llangollen is served by bus no. 94 from Wrexham and Dolgellau. Telephone 01352 704035 for details.

Valle Crucis Abbey

This Cistercian abbey is named after the 'valley of the cross' in which it is situated. The cross may have been 20 feet high, but all that remains is the lower half, known as the Pillar of Eliseg. This has a curious phallic look about it. Llangollen shares St. Collen with Glastonbury and both places have 'castles of the grail'. Miller and Broadhurst have shown in their book 'The Sun and the Serpent' how male and female energy lines meet at Glastonbury and the same would seem to be the case here. An abbey or church dedicated to the cross seems to mark the crossing of male and female energy lines. Suspecting that the original valley cross would be the vital spot, I dowsed there but could only find a male energy line. It led straight to the altar of the ruined abbey, where a female energy line crossed it, having come from a cairn on Eglwyseg Mountain at grid reference SJ 231463. It would seem that the male energy line penetrates a cup (grail?) formed by the female energy lines on Castell Dinas Bran, as they do on Glastonbury Tor. The cross (Eliseg's Pillar) was erected by Cyngen, who died in 854 and was the last of the kings of Powys. The inscription records how he was descended from Magnus

Maximus, the general who led a British army to the continent in AD 383 and, briefly, became the Roman Emperor. That great patriot Owain Glyndŵr is said to have met the Abbot of Valle Crucis on his early morning walk. The Prince remarked that the Abbot had risen early, only for the Abbot to reply that it was Glyndŵr who had risen early – a hundred years too early. One hundred years later, of course, the Tudors were on the throne.

St. Collen is said to have dealt with a giantess who waylaid travellers and ate them on the Bwlch-y-Rhiwfelen. Collen killed her, while he dealt summarily with the fairies too, either here or at Glastonbury Tor or at both places, splashing holy water over them after refusing their hospitality. Collen is also the name for a hazel tree in Welsh, the tree associated with protection from fairies. One man who did meet the fairies on the southern slope of Castell Dinas Bran and dance with them was the shepherd Tudur ap Einion Gloff. He was found next morning spinning like mad.

Valle Crucis Abbey

The Walk

1. Go left from the Tourist Information Centre to cross the bridge over the River Dee and pass Llangollen Railway station on your left. Turn right for 20 yards, then turn left up Wharf Hill. Reach the Llangollen Canal and turn left along its tow path to walk with the canal on your right and above the railway on your left for one and a half miles. When you reach a sign for the Chain Bridge Hotel and Ty Craig is on your left, turn right to cross the canal by a bridge.

2. Go left along a road to where it forks into three. Take the right fork and immediately turn sharply right up steps to follow a path through the National Trust's Coed Hyrddyn (Velvet Hill). Walk above a wooded slope descending to the road on your right. Go ahead over a stile, keep above a fence on your right and bear left around the hillside. Descend to a stile giving access to a road. Go left along the metalled path in its verge to pass above the ruins of Valle Crucis Abbey on your right. Pass a garage on your left and turn sharply right down a lane to reach a telephone box on your left at a junction with the road. Turn left along the road for 100 yards and turn right through a kissing gate to come to Eliseg's Pillar.

3. Return to the road and go left towards the abbey ruins, soon passing the telephone box on your right. Fork left down the signposted access lane to Valle Crucis Abbey. Facing the abbey entrance, bear left down the right-hand side of a caravan park, cross a footbridge over the Eglwyseg River and climb to a signpost. Turn right to take a gate and signposted track back towards Llangollen. Reach a road.

4. Go left along the road and turn left up a lane. Pass Dinbren Road on your left and go ahead as signposted for Llangollen,

with Castell Dinas Bran rising in front of you. Pass a signposted footpath going into woodland on your left, follow the road across a stream and turn left over a stile to take the next signposted path. Walk above the stream on your left and turn right in the corner to climb to a stile in the top corner. Cross it, with Castell Dinas Bran above you.

5. Turn right to walk beside a fence on your right to a kissing gate beside a gate. If you can cope with a strenuous climb to 1062 feet, divert sharply left here along the signposted path to the summit of Castell Dinas Bran, then retrace your steps. Continue through the kissing gate along the signposted path back to Llangollen. Go ahead at a cross-tracks, continue through a kissing gate and go down the left-hand side of sloping pasture. Take a kissing gate in the bottom left corner to follow the enclosed path past a school on your right. Retrace your steps from the canal into Llangollen.

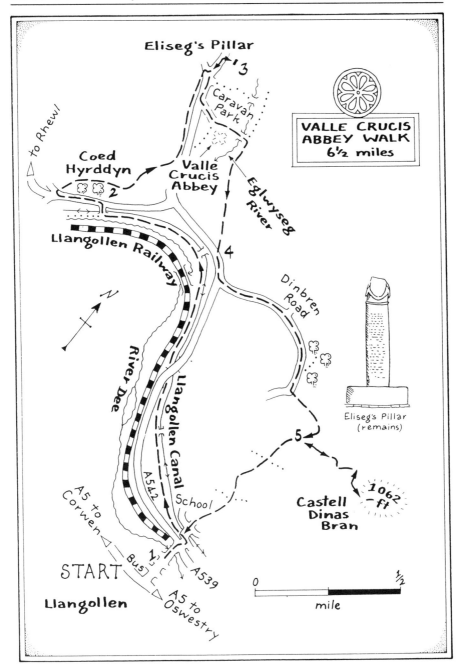

Eliseg's Pillar

Caravan Park

VALLE CRUCIS
ABBEY WALK
6½ miles

to Rhewl

Coed
Hyrddyn

Valle
Crucis
Abbey

Eglwyseg River

Llangollen Railway

N

Dinbren Road

River Dee

Llangollen Canal

Eliseg's Pillar
(remains)

A542

School

Castell
Dinas
Bran

1062
ft

A5 to Corwen

Bus

START

Llangollen

A5 to Oswestry

A539

0   ½

mile

12. Caᴅaiʀ íᴅʀís

Route: Lay-by at the top of the Tal-y-llyn Pass — Mynydd Gwerngraig — Mynydd Moel — Penygadair — Mynydd Moel — Mynydd Gwerngraig — Lay-by at the top of the Tal-y-llyn Pass.

Distance: 7½ miles. Strenuous.

Map: OS Outdoor Leisure 23 Snowdonia — Cadair Idris area.

Start: Lay-by at the top of the Tal-y-llyn Pass (SH 753135).

Access: The lay-by is beside the A487 between Machynlleth and Dolgellau. Bus no. 94A (Aberystwyth — Dolgellau) stops by request if a clear hand signal is given.

Cadair Idris

Respect the 2928ft peak of Cadair Idris because mist could descend suddenly and demand the use of map and compass, as well as sensible clothes, footwear and emergency rations carried in a rucksack. Pack a torch and batteries but don't plan to use it – allow plenty of daylight hours to complete this walk. Take note of features as you ascend so that the descent along the same path is easy to find.

Respect Cadair Idris too because it is a holy mountain. Some say that whoever must govern all of Britain must hold two sacred spots, being the Tower of London and Cadair Idris. Certainly, Dafydd, the brother of Llywelyn the Last, made his final stand against the English on the slopes of Cadair Idris in 1283. The United Kingdom will disintegrate when Cadair Idris is no longer governed by Westminster. Meirionnydd has elected a Plaid Cymru M.P. ever since 1974.

This is a very masculine mountain, so it will love ladies who stay a night on it. Perhaps the giant Idris, whose chair this is, will come to them in their dreams. A great astronomer, astrologer and philosopher, Idris is attended by the Cwn Annwn or Hounds of the Underworld. Do look out for moving 'earth lights' – many have seen them here. Close proximity to such a magical place can cause great stress to humans, so if you do stay a night at the summit you may risk death or madness, on the other hand you could become an inspired poet.

One person who witnessed an 'earth light' here was Paul Devereux, author of *Earth Lights Revelation* (Blandford, 1989). Recalling the incident from 1982, he recorded 'a blue-white ball of light hurling itself across the night sky'. Estimated at being one or two feet across, it must have moved at more than 600 m.p.h.. Paul Devereux's research on 'earth lights' is some of the most valuable in the field of understanding the energies of the living Earth and the old fairy traditions. The Mochras Fault running north from Barmouth to Harlech is linked with some of the best and most well-attested examples of 'earth lights', as Paul Devereux records in detail in his book. Such lights are also seen along the Bala Fault, also overlooked by Cadair Idris, especially in early January. Are these from the Underworld? Are they the Cwn Annwn?

Cadair Idris

The Walk

1. Go left from the lay-by along the road towards Dolgellau.

2. Turn left across a ladder stile beside a gate and climb to join a fence on your left. Walk with it on your left as you ascend, going over a ladder stile in a fence ahead.

3. Bear left with the fence and cross another ladder stile beside a gate in the next fence ahead. As you approach the foot of crags, diverge from the fence to take the steep path up to a plateau. Rejoin the fence on your left.

4. Turn left over a step stile in the corner, then immediately turn right over another step stile. Turn left to continue with this fence on your left.

5. Go ahead over a ladder stile in the corner where the fence ends. Continue up Mynydd Moel. There is one more ladder stile to cross as you make your way along the northern edge of Idris' mighty chair. Take care with the cliffs on your right should there be mist. Go ahead to the summit, ignoring the Fox's Path on your right shortly before it. There is a hut just below the summit cairn.

6. Retrace your steps from the summit, keeping close to the fence after descending from Mynydd Moel. Take care when going down the crags. Go right along the road back to the lay-by.

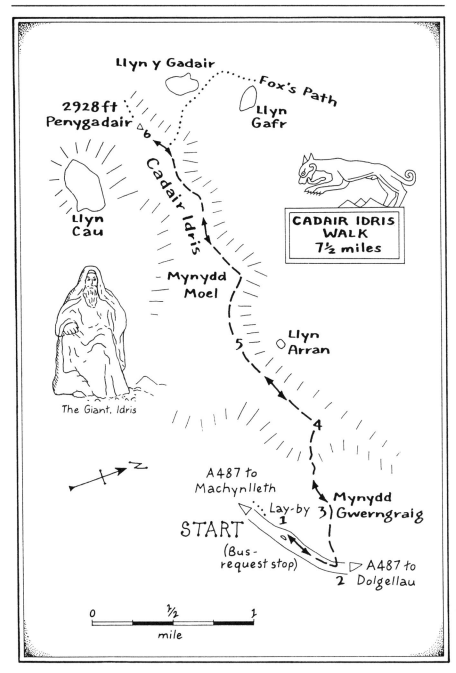

Llyn y Gadair

Fox's Path

2928 ft
Penygadair △6

Llyn
Gafr

Cadair Idris

Llyn
Cau

CADAIR IDRIS
WALK
7½ miles

Mynydd
Moel

Llyn
Arran

5

The Giant, Idris

4

A487 to
Machynlleth

Lay-by 3) Mynydd
1   Gwerngraig

START
(Bus-
request stop)

A487 to
2 Dolgellau

0   ½   1

mile

13. Ôínas mawòôwy

Route: Dinas Mawddwy – Castell – Meirion Mill – Dinas Mawddwy.

Distance: 7 miles. Strenuous.

Map: OS Outdoor Leisure 23 Snowdonia – Cadair Idris area.

Start: The Red Lion Inn (Gwesty'r Llew Coch), Dinas Mawddwy (SH 859148).

Access: Dinas Mawddwy lies below the A470 about 10 miles east of Dolgellau. The Red Lion is on one corner of a road junction at the northern end of the village. There are parking spaces for cars. Buses run to Dinas Mawddwy from Dolgellau (no. 33) and Machynlleth (no. 518), where there is a railway station. Telephone 01286 679535 for details. There is also a bus on Saturdays from Shrewsbury (no. 280) which stops on the A470 at the Buckley Pines Hotel, Dinas Mawddwy (telephone 01654 711291 for details).

Dinas Mawddwy

Mawddwy may be derived from Amwn Ddu, the father of Tydecho, the patron saint of Mawddwy. More likely, however, is its derivation from the Earth Goddess Mawdd, Medb or Maeve. This was the territory of the Gwylliaid Cochion Mawddwy ('Red Bandits of Mawddwy'). The Welsh word 'gwyll' can signify gloom, shade, duskiness, a hag, a witch, a fairy and a goblin. The term is particularly applied to mountain fairies of gloomy or harmful habits, haunting lonely roads to take advantage of travellers. Perhaps the Red Bandits had fairy blood in their veins, or the spirit of the land so possessed them. Whatever they were, they found sanctuary in this sheltered, womb-like spot where the great bulk of the mountains to the west brings an early end to the day's sunshine. The patron saint is Tydecho, a son of Amwn Ddu and a nephew of King Arthur (whose sister, Anne, was Tydecho's mother). He came in conflict with Maelgwn Gwynedd (a candidate for Arthur's Sir Lancelot). First, Maelgwn sent Tydecho horses to graze, to be fed with Tydecho's prayers because the grazing was so poor. The horses throve and changed colour from white to gold. Maelgwn then tried to annoy the saint by stealing the oxen he ploughed with. Tydecho responded by ploughing with stags, while a wolf harrowed behind. Maelgwn then set his dogs on these animals and sat down on a rock to enjoy the sport. He soon found he was stuck to the rock, however. He could only stand up after begging Tydecho's forgiveness, returning his oxen and granting the right of sanctuary to Mawddwy for a hundred ages.

This right of sanctuary and Mawddwy's remoteness from central authority, whilst offering rich pickings from the travellers using the roads through it, led to the Red Bandits making it their base until the reign of Mary Tudor. If 'a hundred ages' equals exactly one thousand years, the right of sanctuary would have been granted in 554 or 555. St. Tydecho's Church at Mallwyd is dated 520, while his mother church at Llanymawddwy would be a year or two older. This gap of about 35 years between the building of the churches and the granting of the right of sanctuary is interesting because it suggests that those who propose that the Celtic Church dated its years from 'the Incarnation of Our Lord' as meaning from the baptism or, perhaps, the crucifixion of Jesus, rather than His birth, might be correct. This was a Gnostic practice.

If we should add thirty-odd years to Celtic dates, the Battle of Camlan was fought around 570, rather than in 537. This would make sense of the Saxon's vital breakthrough against the weakened British at the Battle of Dyrham, north of Bath, in 577 (a Saxon dating, so from what Rome decided was the birth of Jesus). The Battle of Camlan was one of the three unfortunate, frivolous battles of Britain. It was a civil war between Arthur and his nephew Medrawt, who aspired to the throne. It was fought here, just to the south of Dinas Mawddwy, at Maes Camlan. The battle started by accident when a knight was bitten by an adder.

Maes-y-camlan, the battlefield, is in the centre of this picture taken from Bryn Cleifion. It stands on the lower slopes of the 1389 ft Craig y Gamell.

He drew his sword to kill it and, inevitably, the glint of it made others think the fighting had started – and so it did. It was Arthur's last battle, leaving him grievously wounded, Medrawt dead and the Celts unable to resist a future Saxon advance. If Camlan hadn't taken place, Welsh could well still be the language spoken on the streets of London. Camlan needed cleansing and on 4th July, 1994 (there was no significance in the actual day – the sixth century battle was probably fought in November), the reincarnation of King Arthur unveiled a memorial stone, blessed by an Archdruid, in the grounds of the Meirion Mill at the edge of the battlefield. The ceremony included the reciting of this poem:

'On Camlan's field a stone we raise,
That it may wield our note of praise
And lay to rest the adder's work,
With all the woes that strife imparts.
Time has healed the wounds of Arthur,
Forgiven Medrawt for the slaughter.
Together now, with one accord,
We acknowledge Arthur as our Lord.
Truth, honour, justice, must once again
Ride triumphant in his reign.'

Perhaps the first Red Bandits were leftovers from the Battle of Camlan. There certainly was a red-freckled man, Cynwrig Frychgoch, from Mawddwy in the sixth century, according to 'The Dream of Rhonabwy' in 'The Mabinogion'. Their one thousand years or hundred ages were up when Baron Lewis Owen (High Sheriff of Merioneth) had eighty of them killed at Collfryn on Christmas Eve, 1554. The mother of one young outlaw pleaded for his life in vain, then bared her breasts and said that they had given suck to others who would avenge his death within a year. On the significant day in the Celtic calendar of Hallowe'en, 1555, the remaining outlaws had their revenge by ambushing Baron Owen at Llidiart y Barwn ('the baron's gate') on the Welshpool road and washing their hands in his blood. These surviving brigands were soon caught and executed.

When you pass Castell (approaching direction point 5), look out for the ghost of a woman who once owned this property. Her husband had a mistress in another valley and when his wife died he forged her will with her dead hand. A ghostly dead hand then appeared to stop the maid from opening a locked cabinet where her former mistress' favourite crockery was kept. Deciding to leave the house, the husband found the horses wouldn't pull the wagon loaded with furniture until their dead mistress' favourite teapot was taken off it. People soon learned to return anything borrowed from the house within the same day.

The Walk

1. Face the Red Lion Inn, go left and turn right down the minor road towards Llanymawddwy. Turn right across the Common to cross the footbridge over the Afon Dyfi.

2. Turn left to walk upstream with the river on your left. Go ahead through a kissing gate, ignore a gate giving access to a hedged track on your right and go ahead with the riverside path past the wall of the old orchard and garden for the Plas or mansion in Dinas Mawddwy (now knocked down). After crossing the second stile, step over a little stream and turn right up the bank to steps which lead to the corner of a field. Go left, keeping above the trees on your left, until the path leads down a slope back to the river. Continue above the river on your left, going ahead over two stiles to emerge in the corner of a meadow. Continue with the river on your left, ignore a footbridge across it and take a track ahead which passes an empty house (starting to become a ruin) on your right, with a fence on your left. Reach a lane.

3. Bear right along the lane to walk up the valley with the river down below on your left. Come to a farmhouse on your left and turn sharply right up a steep track. Take a gate at the top to go ahead to the farmhouse of Bwlch-coediog.

4. Go down the access lane from Bwlch-coediog and pass the house known as Castell on your right, just after a track leading right. Descend to a gully on your right and turn left opposite this to take an old green lane beside a stream. Go ahead over a ford near an old, broken, footbridge at the confluence with Nant Cwm Cewydd. Turn right with the old green lane which soon bears left uphill and turns right to pass the ruins of Pant-glas

on your left. Continue along the foot of a wooded slope, pass three farmhouses and fork right down to the A458 road.

5. Turn right along the road carefully and bear right up a lane to a junction marked by a letterbox. Turn right to follow a lane up this side valley (Cwm-Cewydd), cross a bridge and follow the lane around a bend on your right.

6. Turn sharply left up an access lane which is signposted as a public footpath. Pass farm buildings on your right, take a gate ahead and walk along the course of the Roman road from Wroxeter to Brithdir, where it linked with Sarn Helen. Turn left over a ladder-stile before the hedged track bears right. Turn right immediately after stepping into the field and go ahead to a stile giving access to woodland. Emerge from this by crossing a stream and a ladder-stile and climbing to rejoin the track. Go left through a gate to continue with a fence on your left. Follow the old Roman road through three more gates.

7. Leave the Roman road as it prepares to bear left downhill. Turn right, as indicated by a yellow waymark arrow on a tree in the hedge ahead and climb with this hedge on your left to a primitive stile in the top corner. Go ahead across this and a step-stile in the next fence, where a splendid view over the battlefield of Camlan unfolds before you. You are now standing on Bryn Cleifion ('the hillside of the bruised – in the sense of wounded'). Bear right to a stile in the fence ahead, halfway up the side of this hill. Bear left down to a stile beside a signpost and take care on a narrow flight of steps leading to the verge of the A470 road. Go right along this verge to cross the modern road bridge over the Afon Dyfi, passing the Meirion Mill (and King Arthur's memorial stone) on your left. Turn right at the Buckley Pines Hotel to follow the access road to Dinas Mawddwy Junior

School, on the line of the old Roman road and the pilgrim's route between St. David's and Holywell.

8. With the school gates on your right ahead, take the kissing gate on your left ahead and follow the signposted public footpath up to the A470. Go right along the pavement and fork right down into the village to return to the Red Lion Inn.

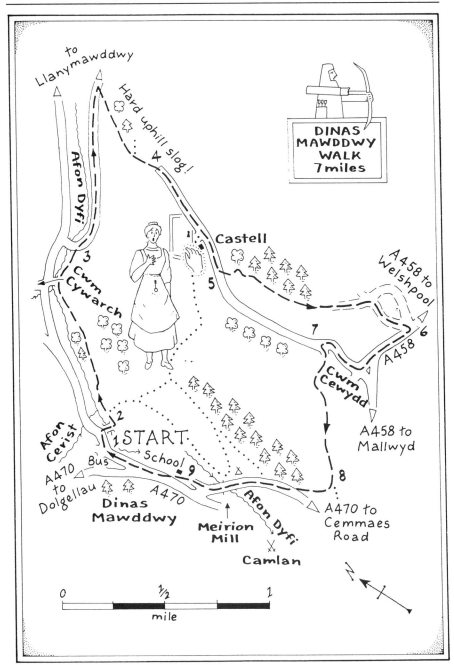

to Llanymawddwy

Hard uphill slog!

4

DINAS
MAWDDWY
WALK
7 miles

Afon Dyfi

Castell

3

Cwm
Cywarch

5

A458 to
Welshpool

7

6

A458

Cwm
Cewydd

A458 to
Mallwyd

Afon
Cerist

2

1 START

School 9

8

A470
to
Dolgellau

A470

Dinas
Mawddwy

Bus

Afon Dyfi

Meirion
Mill

A470 to
Cemmaes
Road

Camlan

0   ½   1

mile

14. cwm maethlon (happy valley)

Route: Snowdonia National Park Car Park, Happy Valley – Llyn Barfog – Carn March Arthur – Cefn-cynhafal – Eglwys Gwyddelod – Erwfaethlon – Snowdonia National Park Car Park, Happy Valley.

Distance: 8 miles. Moderate.

Map: OS Outdoor Leisure 23 Snowdonia – Cadair Idris area.

Start: Snowdonia National Park Car Park, Happy Valley (SN640986).

Access: Cwm Maethlon (Happy Valley) is served by a minor road running between Tywyn and Cwrt. The nearest bus stop is at Cwrt, over one mile east of Pant-yr-on (7), for bus no. 29 (Machynlleth-Tywyn).

Cwm Maethlon (Happy Valley)

This remote, tranquil, valley has nourished human life for thousands of years. Overlooked on both north and south by ancient ridgeways, it is steeped in legend and magical atmosphere.

Llyn Barfog may have acquired its English name, Bearded Lake, because of the water-lilies which cover it every summer. In times past, it was associated with a monster. Either Hu Gadarn (Hugh the Mighty) or King Arthur dealt with it. Hu Gadarn came around 2000 B.C., at the end of the Age of Taurus, and may be the original 'John Bull'. A superhuman figure, he taught much, including the educational system of the druids.

Llyn Barfog is also where a fairy cow came from, providing the farmer at nearby Dysyrnant with rich milk. As it grew old, the ungrateful fool thought to fatten it up for slaughter. When the butcher came to despatch the cow, however, a green lady came from the lake to call the cow home:

Dere di felen Einion,
Cyrn Cyfeiliorn – braith y Llyn,
A'r foel Dodin,
Codwch, dewch adre.

Come yellow Anvil, stray horns,
Speckled one of the lake,
And of the hornless Dodin,
Arise, come home.'

All her progeny, except one, went with her and the farmer was ruined. One cow did remain and she changed colour from white to black. Welsh black cattle are descended from her, while the farmers at Dysyrnant (the farm one mile north of the lake) remain cursed.

Carn March Arthur is where Arthur's horse left an impression of its hoofprint after leaping across the Dyfi estuary. This may be a folk memory of a ley, or spirit path. Two very strong leys cross here and one does come from across the estuary, from Bedd Taliesin. Taliesin, the Chief of Bards and a contemporary of Arthur is buried there (SN 672912). Another ley links Carn March Arthur with Croes faen, the ancient standing stone bearing the later carving of a cross on the edge of Tywyn (SH 597015).

The stone circle above the track at SH663002 is an interesting little ring. Its name, Eglwys Gwyddelod, suggests it was considered to be a place of worship for the Irish who inhabited this part of Wales before Cunedda Wledig came down from north of Hadrian's Wall in the early fifth century.

There were probably eight stones originally but the five remaining large stones (not counting the stone to the north outside the ring, while the large stone to the north-east seems to have been displaced) fit an ellipse exactly. The major axis is 10.5 megalithic yards (2.72ft or 0.829m, after Prof. A. Thom).

There is a minor axis of 9.5 megalithic yards and a distance between the foci of 4.5 (actually 4.47) megalithic yards. The perimeter is very nearly three times the major axis, being 31.3 megalithic yards. Cock fighting was held here in the 19th century.

One night I saw a vision which explained stone circles in a vivid way. I saw Rhiannon, the Fairy Princess and the goddess of Wales. Her cupped hands formed a chalice, containing energy or spirit. She was of the earth, which was coloured orange, while the bones of Rhiannon's fingers and the nerves leading from her were of white, or silver. The energy was dispersed or collected along these, while a corresponding but celestial cup formed a glorious symmetry above. The tips of Rhiannon's fingers were the standing stones which formed the circle. Within it was an interchange of energies, a swirling cauldron of spirit, from above and below. This vision was a privilege, coming with the knowledge that Rhiannon had shown me one of her secrets.

Carn March Arthur

The Walk

1. Take the kissing gate at the back of the car park and turn left along the path to Tyddyn-y-briddell. Bear left to pass the farmhouse on your right and go ahead over a ladder stile to the right of a gate across the path. Ignore a track ascending on your right and go ahead as waymarked by a yellow arrow, continue over another ladder stile, to the left of a gate ahead.

2. Bear right off the firm track where a public footpath signpost directs you up the hillside to a gateway. Go through this (or over the ladder stile to the right of the gate). Continue to Llyn Barfog (Bearded Lake), which is preceded by a gate with a ladder stile in the fence on your left. Walk past the lake on your left to reach a slate waymark post. Turn left to reach a point overlooking a marshy area where, if you shout, an echo will be bounced back to you from the cliff opposite.

3. Retrace your steps past Llyn Barfog, now on your right. Turn left along a path, about 50 yards before the gate and stile encountered as you approached the lake. Reach an old ridgeway track and divert right along it to find Carn March Arthur, on your right just before the start of a stone wall on your left. A slate slab marks the hoofprint in the rock.

4. Retrace your steps from Carn March Arthur overlooking the Dyfi estuary on your right. Go ahead along this old track, going back over a stile beside a gate and ignoring the path on your left which led you from Llyn Barfog. Bear right with the track, go through a gate across it and converge with a track coming from your right.

5. Descend to walk between forestry plantations. Emerge through
    a gate, cross a slab footbridge and reach a wall on your right.
    Leave the track here by bearing left. Pass above farm buildings
    on your left. Fork left, away from Cefn-cynhafal.

6. Take the gate ahead and pay close attention to these direc-
    tions in consultation with the inset map for this section of the
    route. The right of way is obstructed (January, 1995). When
    first surveyed, in 1989, these obstructions were reported to
    Gwynedd County Council together with a suggested diversion
    agreed with the farmer in 1989. The bureaucratic wheels grind
    exceedingly slowly, so this book suggests that you avoid the
    obstructions to the right of way by taking the agreed, if still
    unofficial, diversion. Do look out for waymarks, heed the farmer's
    advice and check on the current state of the right of way.
    Meanwhile, bear right down to a stream, going through two
    gates. Cross it and bear left to a small gate. Turn right through
    this to walk along the foot of a slope beside a stone wall on your
    right. After going through another gate, bear left up bare
    pasture to a gate giving access to the road. Go right along the
    road down to a house on your left.

7. Turn left through a gate just before the house. Climb with a firm
    track, keeping beside a wall on your right. Go through a gate
    and bear right with the track to climb to another gate. Follow
    a muddy track with a fence on your left and soon come to a
    stone circle (Eglwys Gwyddelod) above the track on your right,
    about 150 yards from the gate.

8. Continue along this prehistoric ridgeway track. Cross a stream
    before going through a gate across it. After taking the next
    gate, come to a path junction where you ignore the path going

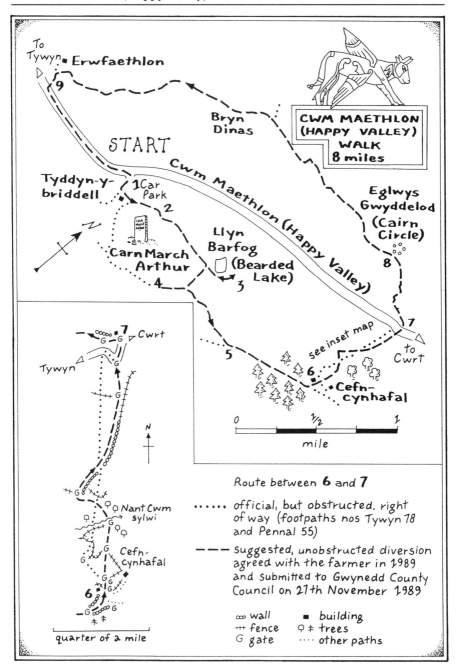

To Tywyn ▷ Erwfaethlon

9

Bryn Dinas

CWM MAETHLON
(HAPPY VALLEY)
WALK
8 miles

START

Cwm Maethlon (Happy Valley)

Tyddyn-y-briddell
1 Car Park
2

Eglwys Gwyddelod
(Cairn Circle)

Llyn Barfog
(Bearded Lake)

Carn March Arthur
4
3

8

7

7
Cwrt
to Cwrt

see inset map

5

Tywyn

6

Cefn-cynhafal

Cefn-cynhafal

0   ½   1
mile

N

++ G
Nant Cwm sylwi

Cefn-cynhafal

6

quarter of a mile

Route between **6** and **7**

· · · · · · official, but obstructed, right of way (footpaths nos Tywyn 78 and Pennal 55)

— — — suggested, unobstructed diversion agreed with the farmer in 1989 and submitted to Gwynedd County Council on 27th November 1989

∞ wall   ▪ building
+++ fence   ⌀⚘ trees
G gate   · · · · other paths

north through a gate in the fence on your right. Bear slightly left as you go ahead to continue through another gate. At the end of this pasture, cross a stile beside the gate ahead to descend towards Erwfaethlon. Turn left with the enclosed path just before this farm and converge with its access track, coming from your right, to go left to the road.

9. Turn left along the road back towards the car park, on your right.

1 ʃ. ᴅɑꞡ Oᴡ eᴅ

Route: Commins Coch – Maen Llwyd, Cefncoch-uchaf – Darowen
– Maen Llwyd, Tal-y-Wern – Darowen – Cwmbychan-mawr –
Commins Coch.

Distance: 7 miles. Moderate.

Map: OS Pathfinder 886 Cemmaes & Llanbrynmair.

Start: Bus Stop, Commins Coch (on A470 near junction with road
up to Darowen, near telephone box and Post Office) (SH 845032).

Access: Commins Coch is on the A470 between Cemmaes Road
and Llanbrynmair. It is served by bus no. 522 from Machynlleth
and Newtown. Telephone 01597 826643 for details.

Darowen

This walk connects the three standing stones forming a sacred
triangle giving sanctuary or 'noddfa'. This does mean the walk is
along lanes, albeit quiet ones. The third stone is no longer
standing and appears to form part of a farmhouse gateway.
Instead of following the lane past this, the alternative of taking a
Forestry Commission track is offered.

The first stone you come to, at Cefncoch-uchaf, is about 3ft 9
ins high and 7ft 6 ins in circumference. Its tip is shaped like the
distant silhouette of Fron Goch, the holy hill towards which it
points. This could be regarded as a 'female' stone.

The second standing stone, near Tal-y-wern, is over 6 feet high
and 12ft 6 ins in circumference. It could be a 'male' stone. It
stands in 'cae yr hen eglwys' (old church field) and there was,
indeed, a hermit's cell near the stone. This stone would appear
to be on a ley or spirit path connecting Croes-faen, near Tywyn,
with the Maengwyn stones outside Lo Cost in Machynlleth and

extending to Cerrig Caerau stone circle above Llanbrynmair (see walk 16).

Perhaps the hermit's cell stood beside the stone for his prayers to give a boost to the spirit flowing along the ley. Hermits are a reminder of Hermes, the Greek god who guided wayfarers on unknown paths, was the messenger of the gods and the leader of departed souls to the other world. In the Middle Ages, Christian hermits were stationed at crucial points for travellers, such as at lighthouses, at fords or ferries, in dense forests and on hilltop beacon sites. Hermes corresponded to the Roman Mercury and the Egyptian Thoth, who seems to be remembered in the Tot or Toot hills of prehistoric Britain.

The easy transition from pagan to Christian function at this site reflects the fact that the druids anticipated the coming of Esse, Esu or Jesus. They welcomed the new religion, with the young Jesus spending a winter at Glastonbury to learn from the druids and to build the first church there. This inspired William Blake's famous poem 'Jerusalem'. Further reading could include 'Celt, Druid and Culdee' by Elder and 'The Drama of the Lost Disciples' by Jowett.

The third stone in the triangle may have stood near grid reference SH 856018. It was blown up in the 19th century and part of it would now appear to help form the gateway at Cwmby-chan-mawr. It was called Carreg y Noddfa. The 'Archaeologica Cambrensis' of 1856 refers to 'the township of Noddfa, the name which implies a place of refuge, or a sanctuary, its limits being properly described by three stones'. Darowen most probably means Owen's Oak, but there could be another meaning to this place name. Could it be derived from Daronwy? Taliesin wrote of Daronwy as affording sanctuary. It is the holy hill (and Darowen does have the holy hill of Fron Goch) providing a refuge above the waters of the great flood. It is 'the rock beyond the billow, to be set in order at dawn, displaying the countenance of Him, who receives the exile into his sanctuary'.

Maen Llwyd, Cefncoch-uchaf

The Walk

1. Take the road signposted for Darowen which goes uphill and passes the telephone box and Post Office on your right. Bear right at a fork to keep climbing. Reach a public footpath signpost on your right and bear right over a waymarked stile. Follow a waymarked track across a stream and bear right uphill to a stile.

2. Cross the stile, turn left and fork right along the higher track to reach a gateway leading to a conifer plantation. Follow the path along the foot of these trees and with a fence on your left. Continue through another gate and fork right uphill through deciduous woodland. Cross a stile and bear right uphill, as waymarked. Cross a stile near the top right-hand corner of this sloping pasture and go left, as waymarked, around the edge of the next field. Reach a waymarked stile in the fence on your left and divert across it to visit the standing stone near Cefncoch-uchaf. There is no right of way to it, so please remember you approach it thanks to the courtesy of the landowner and at your own risk. Return over the stile and go left to resume your previous direction. Turn right with the fence when you come to a corner, pass a house on your left, turn left over a waymarked stile and go ahead along the access track. Ignore a waymarked stile on your right. The landowner has allowed readers of this book to continue along his access track (at their own risk, until an official diversion is effected), so bear left with it to a cross-tracks.

3. Turn left to take the old green lane down towards Darowen. Beware of its bare rock surface. You may have to crawl down some parts, especially in wet weather. Go ahead along the road, first going left when you reach the road at a corner, then bearing right at a junction, descending and then ascending to reach the

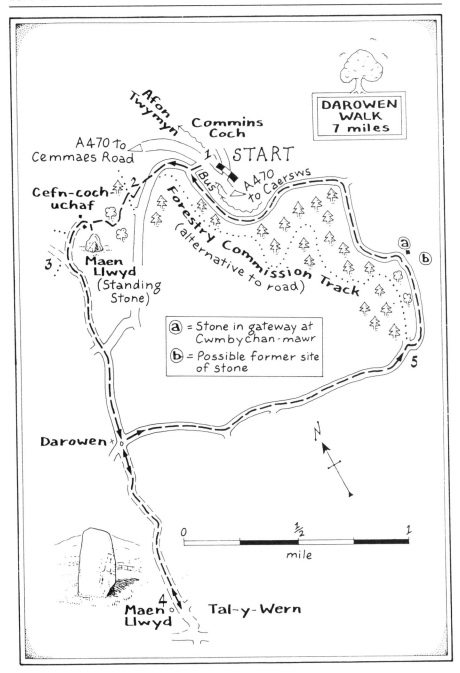

DAROWEN
WALK
7 miles

Afon Twymyn

A470 to Cemmaes Road

Commins Coch

1 START

Bus

A470 to Caersws

Cefn-coch-uchaf 2

Forestry Commission Track (alternative to road)

3 Maen Llwyd (Standing Stone)

ⓐ

ⓑ

5

ⓐ = Stone in gateway at Cwmbychan-mawr

ⓑ = Possible former site of stone

Darowen x

N

0   ½   1
mile

4 Maen Llwyd   Tal-y-Wern

village. Ignore the lane on your left, although you will return to it. Go ahead a few yards and turn left down a lane which is signposted as a public footpath. Its surface deteriorates to that of a track. Follow it for about one mile and come to a junction with a track on your left. This is where the gate on your right gives access to the field containing the second standing stone, near Tal-y-Wern. Again, this standing stone is on private land.

4. Retrace your steps to Darowen and this time take the lane on your right which was on your left when you ignored it upon entering the village.

5. If you don't mind missing the remnant of the third stone and wish to leave the road, turn left along the Forestry Commission track which leads through a forest back to the road by which you climbed up from Commins Coch. Turn right down this to the start. If you do remain on the road, pass Cwmbychan-mawr, with part of the third standing stone in its gateway, on your right and follow the road as it curves left back to Commins Coch.

16. LLanBRynmaír

Route: Llanbrynmair – Tafolwern – Cringoed – Llan – Bont Dolgadfan – Cerrig Caerau and Lled Croen-yr-ych stone circles – Ty-mawr – Llanbrynmair.

Distance: 7 miles. Strenuous.

Maps: O.S. Pathfinders 886 Cemmaes & Llanbrynmair and 907 Penffordd-Las.

Start: The car park beside the A470 in Llanbrynmair (SH 898028).

Access: Llanbrynmair is on the A470 between Cemmaes Road and Caersws, at its junction with the B4518. Bus no. 522 stops here between Newtown and Machynlleth (tel. 01970 617951 for times).

The Stone Circles above Llanbrynmair

Why did our ancestors erect stone circles, particularly at such inconvenient spots as on top of a 1300 ft plateau? The views are inspiring, of course, while the heavens seem much closer. Pumlumon Fawr, the great holy mountain near the centre of Wales, seems especially linked to this place, while leys can be discerned going in other directions. Theories abound, from those expounded by Alexander Thom in his 'Megalithic Sites in Britain' to George Terence Meaden's ideas in 'The Goddess of the Stones'. The name of the second of these two circles may give us a clue. Lled Croen-yr-ych translates into English as 'width of the ox hide'. The local legend is that the stones mark the circumference of an ox hide when spread on the ground.

There is another local legend about an ox being tethered here and a cow being tethered on another peak and the two bellowing to each other. That probably refers to a ley or spirit path between

the two places. The reference to the ox hide is even more interesting. Shamans or prehistoric holy men used to lie down on an
ox hide in order to gain visions. 'The Dream of Rhonabwy' in 'The
Mabinogion' begins with Rhonabwy going to sleep on a yellow
ox skin. Presumably, holy men would lie down within this circle
in order to dream. If so, these stones must mark a very special
place on Mother Earth. The navel is the place to contemplate and
the story of 'Lludd and Llefelys' in 'The Mabinogion' describes
Oxford as the navel of Britain. Oxford is known for its 'dreaming
spires'. To dream is to enter other dimensions, most easily
achieved at sacred spots and at certain times. The veil between
the worlds must be thin here. When a friend rested here, she had
a vision of a ceremony which appeared to date from the 14th or
15th century AD. Hooded figures had blue crosses embroidered
on their chests. Who knows what went on here (and it was by full
moon) not that long ago?

I've yet to sleep here, but one night at Carningli I was privileged
with a special dream which seems relevant. The Goddess, whom
I take to be Rhiannon, cupped her hands. The scene shifted so
that her hands were in the earth, which was a vivid orange, while
her bones were a brilliant white. Other white lines were going
from or to her cupped hands, as if channelling spirit or energy
through the ground. Above her hands was a beautiful symmetry
of a celestial dome, the whole forming a cauldron which con-
tained a whirling spiral of energy or spirit, as if an interchange
was taking place between the earth and the sky. Then the picture
zoomed in on the tips of her fingers, which stuck out of the ground
in a circle (in cross section in the dream, so only a semi-circle
was in view). The tips of Rhiannon's fingers were the standing
stones of a stone circle.

The Walk

1. Go left along the A470 road, cross a bridge over a river and reach a signposted public footpath on your left. Turn left through a kissing gate into the corner of a field. Keep to the left of a line of poles and continue across a stile, cut across the corner of the next field to go over another waymarked stile and turn right to walk with a hedge on your right. Pass a fieldgate but turn right through a waymarked kissing gate. Keep to the right-hand edge of this field but bear slightly left to take another kissing gate in the fence ahead and bear left, as waymarked. Go down the access track of the sewage works to meet a road at Tafolwern. Turn left at the T-junction marked by a telephone box, cross a bridge over a river, fork right and pass the old castle mound (Domen Fawr) on your left. Follow the No Through Road ahead over a bridge across the Afon Twymyn.

2. Turn left at Ty-canol and take the left-hand of two tracks entering the farmyard, passing the old farmhouse on your left. Reach two gates and take the right-hand one to pass an outbuilding on your right and follow a firm track up the hillside. Watch out for a gate facing you where there is a projected corner in the fence on your left and the track bears right around it. Take this gate to continue across pasture and through a gate in the fence ahead. Walk along the top of the next three fields, going over a waymarked stile, through a gate and emerging through another gate in the neck of a field. Go ahead down to the buildings of Cringoed.

3. Turn left through a gate across Cringoed's access lane and immediately turn sharply right along another track for a short distance. Turn left down a gully between two small paddocks and keep near the fence on your right as you descend to a stream. Ford the stream and go straight up the wooded slope

ahead. Cross a firm track and aim just to the left of the church on top of the hill ahead. A stile has been requested for the next fence, where the right of way crosses it to give access to the corner of the field ahead on your right. Go up the left-hand edge of this field and go through gates before turning left just before the church to join the B4518 road. Turn right along this to pass below St. Mary's Church, Llan, on your right.

4. Notice a public footpath signpost on your right pointing across the road to your left. Bear left through a waymarked gate. Pass a garden on your right, cross a stile to enter a field and bear right downhill. Cross a narrow second field, continue over a firm track in a third field and cross a footbridge over a stream shaded by trees. Follow the path around to Bethel Chapel and bear left down to the road in Bont Dolgadfan.

Looking back from the path approaching Llan church

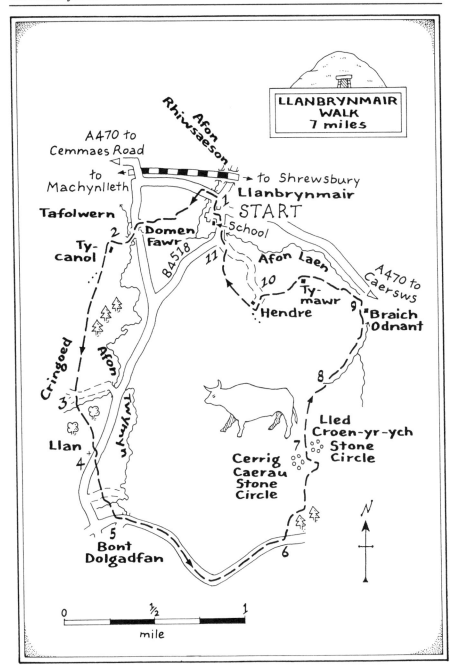

5. Go left along the road, cross a bridge over the Afon Twymyn and follow the road uphill.

6. Reach a public footpath signpost on your right which points across the road to your left. Turn left along this path, going through a gate and past a pond on your left. Bear right to go through a gate onto the bare hillside, keeping above a small plantation of conifers on your right. Approach a valley and bear left to climb above it. Diverge from the right of way shown on the O.S. map by bearing right to the corner formed by a fence ahead and a fence on your right. This is where the waymarked stile is that allows you to cross the fence. Bear left over it to reach another waymarked stile in the fence ahead on your right, just to the right of Cerrig Caerau stone circle.

7. Cross the stile beside the stone circle and bear right about 135 yards to the second stone circle (Lled Croen-yr-ych). This is on private land, so respect the courtesy of the farmer and retrace your steps to the stile beside the first stone circle to rejoin the right of way. Bear right, as indicated by a waymark arrow (left if you were coming over the stile, without having diverted to the second stone circle). Reach a gate in the left-hand corner ahead and either go through it or go over the stile in the fence to its right. Bear very slightly right to cross the moorland plateau and reach a fence ahead. Look for a yellow waymark arrow on this which instructs you to bear right downhill, beside the fence on your left.

8. Turn left over a stile in the fence, step across a stream and go down a ravine, keeping the stream on your right. Approach a farmhouse (Braich-Odnant) and turn left before it to walk with its fence on your right. Go through a gate into a field and bear right beside the fence on your right down to a waymarked gate. Go through this to follow a track for a few yards.

9. Turn left across a stile to return to the field and go ahead, as waymarked, along the bottom of this pasture above a river on your right. Enter a second field and bear slightly left, keeping above the meadow. Go ahead into the next field, where you gradually converge with a fence on your left. Continue along an enclosed path to pass below the farmhouse of Ty-mawr on your left. Fork left to pass farm buildings on your left. Turn right through a gateway and go along the left-hand edge of this field. Take the gate in the corner and follow the path across the next field to a stile beside a gate giving access to a lane.

10. Turn left up the lane to pass a farmhouse on your right. Turn right, before the farm outbuildings. Descend to a waymarked gap in a line of trees and walk along the right-hand edge of the next field. Cross a stile in the corner ahead, keep to the left-hand edge of this field and continue over another stile to walk along the left-hand edge of the following field. Cross a stile in the corner and go ahead, as waymarked, to cross a stile in a fence on your right and go left down a track to a road.

11. Turn right along the road to pass the school in Llanbrynmair on your left, then turn left down the access and car park for the community centre to take a path at the end and turn right along Glan Clegyr. Ignore a turning on your right, go ahead past bungalows on your left and continue to the car park.

17. montgomery

Route: Montgomery – Lymore – Offa's Dyke – Montgomery.

Distance: 4 miles. Easy.

Map: OS Pathfinder 909 Montgomery.

Start: Broad Street, Montgomery (SO 223964).

Access: Montgomery is at the junction of the B4385 with the B4386 and the B4388 some six miles south of Welshpool. For details of bus services, including from Shrewsbury, telephone 01597 826643.

The Robber's Grave, Montgomery

John Newton Davies was engaged as the bailiff of Oakfield Farm, near Montgomery, by the rich widow of James Morris around 1819. He not only made the farm prosperous but fell in love with Mrs. Morris' daughter. This didn't suit Robert Parker, who had designs on the farm, and Thomas Pearce, who desired the girl. They set John Newton Davies up by committing a robbery and giving the impression that it was the bailiff's work. One account is that a watch worth 30/- (£1.50) and one shilling in change (5p) were stolen. For this, the bailiff was tried and condemned to death, in November, 1821. As he stood on the scaffold, which may have been behind Montgomery's town hall, he swore his innocence and predicted that Nature would provide proof by not allowing any grass to grow on his grave for at least one generation. It was reliably reported that there was still a bare patch on his grave over one hundred years after his execution, which was attended by a sudden mighty thunderstorm. A man who planted a rosebush on the grave came to an untimely end, while Thomas Pearce was killed in a quarry explosion and Robert Parker died of a wasting disease. Dowsing suggests that the grave is on a spirit path linking it with the 1700 ft summit of Corndon Hill, to the east.

The Robber's Grave

The Walk

1. With your back to the town hall, go down Broad Street, across a road and straight up Church Bank. Go left into the church-yard, pass the church on your right and aim for the gate at the far (northern side) of the churchyard. As you approach this, some 15 yards from the gate, go about 15 yards on your left to find the Robber's Grave, marked with a sign and with a rosebush intertwined with a holly tree now growing from it. Return to Church Bank, go left to resume your previous direction and turn right at a junction to pass Spider Cottage on your left and pass a house which stands on the site of the old town ditch (Clawdd y Dre). This house is dated 1726. Bear right down Lions Bank.

2. Turn left along a road and pass a children's playground on your left. Continue past a patch of woodland on your left and turn left through a gate to follow a signposted bridleway. Go ahead along the left-hand side of two fields.

3. Bear right along a metalled lane, ignore a track forking right to a house, which is passed on your right. Go ahead with the metalled lane past a cricket ground on your left, over a cattle grid and with a fence on your right. Go ahead over another cattle grid to follow the lane through woodland. Emerge from this to approach another cattle grid.

4. Cross the cattle grid and immediately turn left along the waymarked Offa's Dyke Path. Walk with a high hedge on your left and the English countryside rolling away to your right. Go ahead over two stiles, reach the end of woodland on your left and cross another stile to continue along the right-hand edge of this field. A well-preserved section of Offa's Dyke leads the rest of the way to the B4386 road.

5. Turn left along the road back into Wales and Montgomery. Bear left with Princes Street to return to Broad Street, on your right.

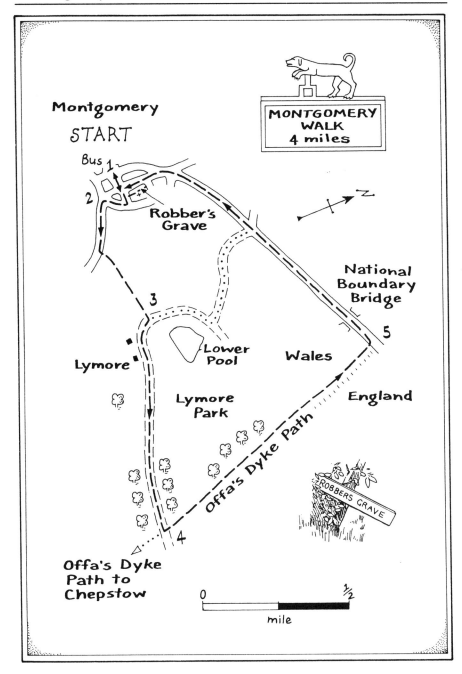

18. nevern

Route: Pont Clydach — Tycanol Woods — Pentre Ifan Burial Chamber — Felindre — Nevern Church — Pilgrims' Cross — Pont Clydach.

Distance: 8½ miles. Easy.

Maps: O.S. Pathfinders 1010 Cardigan & Dinas Head and 1033 Newport & Eglwyswrw.

Start: Pont Clydach lay-by beside the A487 one mile east of Newport (SN 071390).

Access: The no. 412 bus (Cardigan — Newport — Fishguard — Haverfordwest) will stop at the start of this walk if clearly requested (tel. 01267 231817 for times). Pont Clydach is on the main A487 road between Fishguard and Cardigan.

Nevern's Crosses

Nevern's church, dedicated to St. Brynach, has the most spiritual atmosphere of any Christian church I have encountered in Wales. There is a very, very special sanctity about it. A guidebook to the church is available. The finely carved 11th century Celtic cross in the churchyard is where tradition states that the cuckoo's song is to be first heard in Pembrokeshire on 7th April, St. Brynach's Day. In the old days the priest wouldn't start the service until the cuckoo had been heard. One year it was very, very late. It did arrive in the end, however, only to die from exhaustion after performing its annual task.

Also in the churchyard is a bleeding yew tree. As you enter, this is the second tree on your right. It is said that a monk was hanged on this tree and before dying swore that the tree would bleed to prove that he really was innocent. A major ley or spirit path goes from the Celtic cross past the bleeding tree and to the summit of Carningli, where St. Brynach communed with the angels in the sixth century. It is said that on Christmas Eve the Star of Bethlehem rises over Carningli to shine onto the Pilgrim's Cross, which is around the corner from the church at Nevern. This cross is carved in the rock above a cave, blocked by a mighty boulder so that you wouldn't notice it without investigating. Before I knew about this cave or the Christmas legend, I recorded a dream on Carningli in which an angel-child (in this case, female) was born to an old woman in a cave, the direction of which was towards Nevern. It is said that Nevern's church was built after St. Brynach had had a vision of a white sow giving birth here. This dream is part of ongoing research at Carningli which will be written up in a future book. This route also goes through Tycanol Woods, where Pan has been seen and where, at a secret spot which the author doesn't wish to reveal here, St. Brynach lived in a cave (with, perhaps, a nearby cave occupied by a mysterious dark-haired lady). Pentre Ifan burial chamber is another magical place, connected to the spot where St. Brynach had his visions and where the current dreamwork takes place at the summit of Carningli by a ley or spirit path.

Carningli's peak is framed by Pentre Ifan burial chamber

The Walk

1. Go up the waymarked steps at the eastern end of the lay-by and cross a stile to enter a field at its corner. Go up the left-hand edge of this field, soon joining a track which swings in from your right. Notice a standing stone in the field, probably aligned with the summit of Carningli, which is to your right ahead. Turn left through a gate in the top left-hand corner and bear left along an old green lane. Go ahead through a metal gate. Go straight ahead at a crosspaths and descend into Cwm Clydach.

2. Turn left, as signposted, towards the Afon Clydach. Cross it by a footbridge and climb up the eastern side of the valley. Follow the path through a small gate and turn right downhill to cross the river again by another footbridge. Bear left to walk with the river on your left, upstream. Walk above the trees, as signposted. Go ahead through delightful woodland, following the waymark posts. Cross a stile in the fence ahead, continue through a field adorned by gorse bushes, with Carningli's angel profile on your right. Go ahead over a ladder stile and eventually emerge over another such stile on an old green lane.

3. Go left down the lane, cross the river by a footbridge beside a ford and continue to a crossroads. Turn left, as signposted for Nevern.

4. Turn right along a track signposted for Fachongle-ganol. Pass this place on your right as you go ahead with the track towards Fachongle-uchaf. Do not take the right of way which goes right through the farmyard, as shown on the O.S. map. Follow the waymarked alternative by turning left through a gate and bearing right down the right-hand edge of a field to a stile. Turn right across this and bear left to walk towards the natural

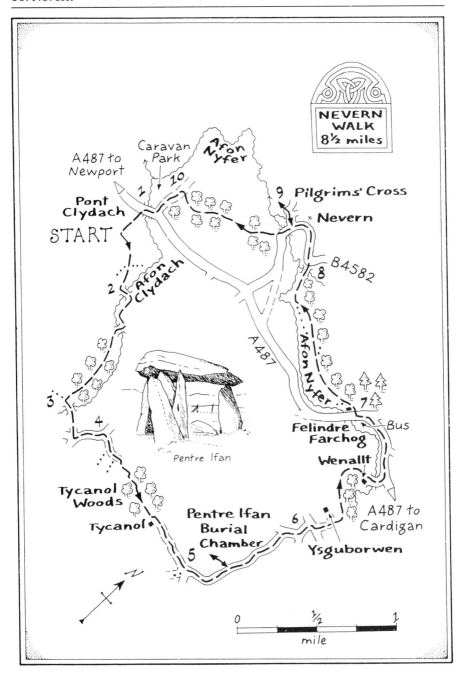

NEVERN
WALK
8½ miles

A487 to
Newport

Caravan
Park

Afon
Nyfer

Pont
Clydach

9 Pilgrims' Cross

× Nevern

START

Afon
Clydach

B4582

8

A487

Afon
Nyfer

7

Bus

Felindre
Farchog

Wenallt

Pentre Ifan

A487 to
Cardigan

Tycanol
Woods

Tycanol

Pentre Ifan
Burial
Chamber

6

Ysguborwen

5

0   ½   1
mile

woodland of Ty Canol. Bear right as you approach the wood to come to a stile giving access into it. Cross this and a subsequent stile. Go ahead along the waymarked path through the wood, soon bearing right. When you approach a gap in a wall ahead, turn left along a waymarked path just before it. Walk with the wall on your right and turn right, as waymarked, with what is now a fence on your right. Pass the buildings of Ty Canol on your right and go ahead along its access track.

5. Reach the corner of a road and turn left along it. Pass a lay-by on your left and take the kissing gate at its northern end to follow the access path to Pentre Ifan burial chamber. Retrace your steps to the road and resume your former direction by going left down it. Follow the road as it bends right when a farm track joins it from your left. Keep left when another road joins yours from your right.

6. Turn right at a T-junction and, in about 100 yards, turn left along a hedged track. When the main track bears left to the farm at Ysguborwen, keep straight ahead through a gate. Descend and bear left above the wooded valley of the Afon Nyfer on your right. Follow the hedged track as it descends and bears right to Wenallt. Continue along this farmhouse's access lane to reach the A487 road. Cross this carefully and turn left along the grassy verge into Felindre Farchog.

7. Fork right just before the Salutation Inn. Follow a track which keeps to the foot of a wooded slope on your right, with the Afon Nyfer away to your left. Go through a gate to enter a nature reserve and fork right, as waymarked. Keep to the lower path, on your left, at the next fork. Reach a signpost and fork right along the path at the foot of the woodland, rather than taking the meadow path. Eventually reach the B4582 road.

8. Go left along the road to pass Nevern's church on your right. After visiting this, turn right over the bridge and follow the road around to a hairpin bend where you take the signposted public footpath on your left for about 35 yards to find the Pilgrims' Cross carved in a cliff on your right.

9. Retrace your steps to the road and the bridge in Nevern. Cross it to approach the telephone box and turn right to cross a bridge over the Afon Nyfer and, just before the first building on your right, turn right over a stile to take a signposted path through a meadow. Continue over a stile to the right of a gate to take a fenced path through a belt of woodland. Go ahead along a woodland track.

10. Turn sharply left along a lane to pass a caravan park on your right, with Carningli ahead on your right. Emerge on the A487 and turn right to reach the lay-by on your left, just after Pont Clydach.

19. Fɾenní Fɑwɾ

Route: Roadside signpost east of Crymych – Castellan Farm – Dol-Newydd – Cilgoed-fach – Frenni Fawr Plantation – Frenni Fawr – Roadside east of Crymych.

Distance: 6 miles. Moderate.

Maps: OS Pathfinders 1033 Newport & Eglwyswrw and 1034 Boncath.

Start: Roadside signpost one and a half miles east of Crymych on the road going towards Bwlchygroes (SN 205343).

Access: Crymych is on the A478 between Cardigan and Narberth. Bus no. 430 runs infrequently from Cardigan to Crymych. Telephone 01267 231817 for timetable information. Take the minor road going east from the northern edge of Crymych, towards Bwlchygroes, for about one and a half miles, to the first signposted public bridleway on your left, opposite a No Through Road on your right.

The Fairies of Frenni Fawr

Most readers won't believe in fairies. One or two of you might. Take it from me that they exist. I've spoken to them on Carningli, but they didn't introduce themselves until I'd slept about forty nights on that mystic mountain. If you happen to spend the night there, you'll have the chance of enjoying a magical sunrise with the Golden Road along the ridge of the Preselis terminating with the peak of Foel Drygarn before the valley containing Crymych. Then there is one more peak, probably rising out of the early morning mist, standing sentinel at the eastern end of these magical hills. This is Frenni Fawr, 1297 feet high and the abode of fairies.

That great recorder of folklore, Wirt Sikes, the United States consul for Wales, set down this tale in his book *British Goblins* (first published in 1880, with a dedication to Albert Edward, Prince of Wales). It is about a shepherd who spotted the fairies dancing in a ring on Frenni Fawr and set out to join in their revelry.

Elegant little ladies wore bright white or vivid scarlet dresses and rode small white horses, while men wore red tripled caps. The shepherd could see the harps but couldn't hear their music until he set foot inside the fairy ring. Seductive melodies led him to a palace full of every beauty and pleasure. There was just one condition to restrict his freedom to enjoy the very best in wine, women and song. He wasn't allowed to drink from a well containing goldfish. Of course, like Eve and the apple, he did this, only to see the fairy realm vanish and to be left shivering on a desolate mountain.

Ley hunters around Cerrig Gaeran stone circle, Llanbrynmair

The Walk

1. There is usually space for a car to be parked considerately beside the road from Crymych to Bwlchygroes about one and a half miles east of Crymych, where a signposted public bridleway leads northwards (on your left if coming from Crymych), opposite a No Through Road. Go north, along the bridleway. This firm, broad, track, is enclosed to begin with. Cross a stile to the right of a gate across it. Bear left, as waymarked by a blue arrow. Continue over another stile beside a gate and emerge from the fenced path by crossing a third stile to the left of a gate ahead. Continue, as waymarked by a blue arrow, across open pasture. Bear slightly right to reach a stile to the right of a gate in the fence ahead.

2. Cross the stile and walk around the foot of the open hillside of Frenni Fawr on your right, keeping near a fence on your left. When you reach the far corner, where a fence comes from your right, go ahead through a waymarked gateway to follow a very wide fenced path.

3. Cross a stile to the right of and above a gate ahead. Descend with the fenced track to reach a lane at a corner where there is a public bridleway signpost. Turn right along this lane. Pass Castellan Farm on your left. When the metalled lane ends, go ahead up the signposted public bridleway. Follow a waymarked track around to a farm.

4. Pass the farmhouse (Dol-newydd) on your right, continue through a small metal gate waymarked by a blue arrow and walk along the bottom, left-hand, edge of a field. Turn left over a stile in the corner and immediately cross a small footbridge. Go down the left-hand side of this second field. A line of trees shields the path on your right, halfway down.

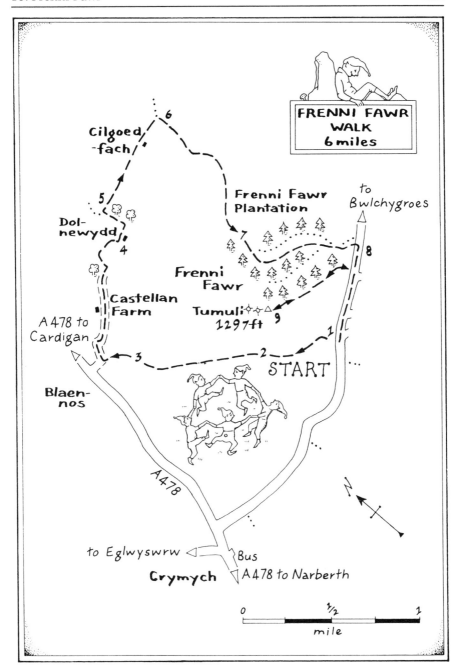

5. Turn right, as waymarked, in the corner. Walk with the hedge on your left along the foot of a field. Continue through a gate and across the next field to a waymarked stile to the left of a gate in the hedge ahead. Keep to the left-hand edge of the following field, go over a stile to the right of the next gate and pass Cilgoed Fach on your right as you take a hedged track ahead.

6. Turn right to ascend with a firm, hedged, track. Cross a stile to the left of the gate at its top and turn left, as waymarked, to walk around the pasture, initially with a hedge on your left. Go ahead over a stile to the right of a gate and follow the track as it contours around the hillside. Go ahead over a waymarked stile beside another gate and head for a forest.

7. Take a gate into the forest. Follow the bridleway, waymarked with a blue arrow, soon bearing right uphill at a fork. Just after going through a gate at the end of the forest, leave the track by turning right over a waymarked stile beside a small wooden gate. Turn left immediately to walk along the left-hand edge of a field to a stile which gives access to the road near a signpost.

8. Turn right along the road for about 300 yards, where a road comes from your left to form a T-junction. Turn right here up the waymarked path which keeps close to a fence on your right. Cross a stile above a gate in the fence and keep climbing, with the forest away to your right. As you climb, your path gradually converges with both the forest on your right and a fence which comes up from your left. Cross a stile in the tip of this field to reach the 1297 ft summit of Frenni Fawr.

9. Retrace your steps downhill to the road and turn right along it back to the signposted public bridleway at the start of this route.

20. LLyn y fan fach

Route: Car Park – Llyn y Fan Fach – Bannau Sir Gaer – Car Park.

Distance: 5½ miles. Strenuous.

Map: OS Outdoor Leisure 12 Brecon Beacons – Western area.

Start: A remote car parking space at grid reference SN 798238.

Access: You'll need the OS map! The nearest railway station is on the Heart of Wales (Swansea – Shrewsbury) Line at Llangadog, some nine miles to the west. Take the A4069 south from there for nearly four miles to Pont-ar-llechau, where you turn east along lanes to Llanddeusant, where the youth hostel might be convenient. Continue east for nearly two more miles until a sign warns you not to proceed along the track. Park above the river on your right, just before a bridge across a tributary stream.

The White Lady of the Lake

There was once a widow's son called Gwyn who tended the family's cattle near Llyn y Fan Fach. One day he was astonished to see the most beautiful young lady in the world standing in the water combing her hair, using its smooth surface as a mirror. He immediately fell in love with her and offered her the bread his mother had given him for lunch. The beauty glided towards him, remarked on the hard-baked bread, said he wouldn't find it easy to catch her and plunged out of sight. Gwyn returned the next day with unbaked dough, only for it to be refused as too moist. The third day he went with half-baked bread and this time she accepted his gift. Gwyn asked her to marry him and she assented on condition that she would leave him after he gave her three causeless blows. He then encountered her father, who said he would consent to their union if he could identify her from her identical sister, which he managed to do because he had earlier noticed how his love had tied her shoe in a peculiar way.

The White Lady of the Lake brought a dowry of cattle, sheep and other animals and the happy couple settled at the farm of Esgair Llaethdy, where they lived happily for many years and brought up three sons. When the eldest was seven, Gwyn and Nelferch (the name of the White Lady from the Lake) were invited to a wedding. They started to walk, then Nelferch decided it was too far and she would ride one of the horses grazing in the field they had reached. Gwyn returned home for her saddle, bridle and gloves and playfully flicked her with the gloves to hurry her into saddling a horse and proceeding. This was the first causeless blow.

Several years later, they were both invited to a Christening. While the other guests were jovial, Nelferch wept because she could see that the infant would have a life of suffering. Gwyn tapped on her shoulder to perk her up – and gave the second causeless blow.

Some time later, the baby they had seen Christened died and they attended its funeral. Whilst others mourned, Nelferch was merry, because the baby was now free of pain. Her husband was shocked and touched her just enough for her to point out that he had given the third causeless blow and that she must leave him for ever, returning with her dowry to the fairy world beneath the waters of the lake. Gwyn drowned himself in the lake in his despair, while their sons were granted a final visit from their mother who instructed them to be healers, showing them the herbs in Pant y Meddygon ('Physicians' Dingle'). The Physicians of Myddfai and their descendants were reckoned to be the best doctors in Wales.

The Walk

1. Having parked any cars at the parking area between the river and the waterboard track just before a notice saying 'Welsh Water Authority No Unauthorised Vehicle Beyond This Point', continue by foot along the track, upstream with the river on your right. Soon cross a bridge over a tributary stream flowing from your left. Bear right with the firm track. Pass another tributary stream on your left. Reach filter beds, where you take a gap in the wall on your left and turn right to walk past the filter beds on your right before rejoining the track. Continue across a bridge over the river and follow the track up to the lake of Llyn y Fan Fach.

The ridge of Bannau Sir Gaer

2. Turn right to walk with the lake down below on your left and up an obvious path to the ridge overlooking the lake. Bear left along the ridge, following a well-trodden path and high above the lake.

3. Continue past the cairn on the 2457 ft summit of Bannau Sir Gaer. Reach a gully on your left and descend carefully with a steep path, perhaps going down the grassy slope on your backside.

4. Bear right initially, below Fan Foel on your right. Bear left across moorland back to the waterboard track.

5. Converge with the outward track near the filter beds and turn right along it to retrace your steps to the car parking area.

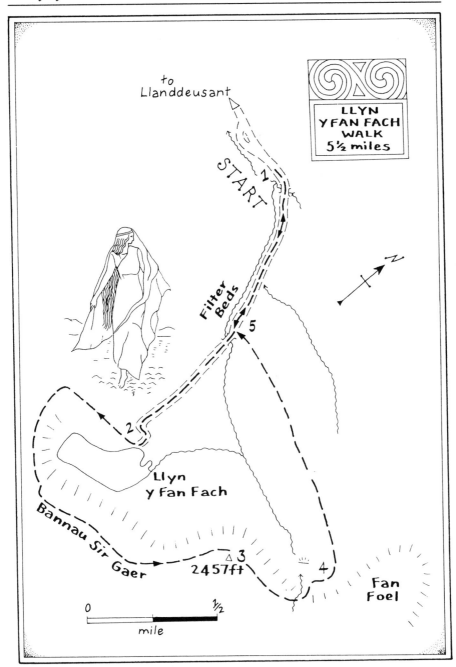

to
Llanddeusant

LLYN
Y FAN FACH
WALK
5½ miles

START

N

Filter
Beds

5

2

Llyn
y Fan Fach

Bannau Sir Gaer

△ 3
2457ft

4

Fan
Foel

0   ½
mile

21. kíౖwelly

Route: Kidwelly Castle – Summer Way – Overlooking Maes Gwenllian – Kidwelly Castle.

Distance: 3½ miles.

Map: OS Pathfinder 1106 Llanelli (North).

Start: Kidwelly Castle (SN 409071).

Access: Kidwelly is on the A484 between Carmarthen and Llanelli. There is a railway station served by trains from Carmarthen and Swansea, while bus services run from several directions. Telephone 01267 231817 for details.

The Ghost of Gwenllian

This is one of the most stirring ghost stories in Wales. Gwenllian was the daughter of Gruffudd ap Cynan, King of Gwynedd and wife of Gruffudd ap Rhys, King of Deheubarth (Dyfed). Her brother was the great Owain Gwynedd. This was in the early 12th century, when Wales was clinging to a tenuous independence. The start of 1136 had raised Welsh hopes with a famous victory over the Norman invaders at Loughor. This encouraged Gruffudd ap Rhys to seek support from his father-in-law in Gwynedd and to drive the hated Normans out of the land they had taken.

The Normans controlled Kidwelly and their Lord Maurice de Londres took advantage of Gruffud ap Rhys' absence in the north to counter-attack. Gwenllian took hold of the situation and, like Boadicea before her, threw herself into the fight. She marched on Kidwelly, where the castle was the centre of Norman power.

About one mile north of the castle, at Maes Gwenllian, she met her death and her army was defeated. A few months later her brother, Owain Gwynedd, was to avenge her death at Crug Mawr, near Cardigan, while her son, Rhys ap Gruffudd, captured the castle at Kidwelly by the 1170s and extended his authority right across South Wales.

Gwenllian's headless ghost was seen walking the battlefield, however, until one night a kind soul was able to reunite it with its head. Another female ghost haunted Pont Spwdwr, two miles east of Kidwelly, on the B4308. This was the shade of Nest, daughter of Sir Elidir Ddu, Lord of Kidwelly at the time of the Crusades. Nest loved Sir Walter Mansel, who returned her love. She had a wicked rival in her cousin Gwladys, however, who found out where the lovers met (in secret, because her father had banned the Norman from his castle before going away on a Crusade). Gwladys tipped off Nest's brother Gruffudd, who had Sir Walter killed by an evil accomplice called Merig, who fired an arrow at him as he met Nest on the bridge. Merig then threw Sir Walter's body into the river. Nest jumped in after it and, as a suicide, was doomed to walk the earth. Release finally came when one of her father's descendants finally did marry a member of the Mansel family.

Kidwelly Castle

The Walk

1. Face the entrance to the castle and go left. Pass the Old Moat House on your left. Turn right at a crossroads to follow the pavement of Water Street. Pass a signposted public footpath for Bwlch-y-Wal on your left.

2. Turn left up the signposted path 'Ffordd yr Haf/Summer Way'. Go straight ahead when the initial firm lane bends left. Climb with the old green lane. Reach a corner where there is a stile and a signpost on your left. Turn right along 'Ffordd yr Haf/Summer Way'.

3. Go through a kissing gate and bear left, as signposted. Climb to the top right-hand corner of this field and turn right to follow the enclosed path with a fence and a field on your left and a hedge on your right. Cross the stile at the end of this enclosed path and bear right, as signposted. Bear slightly left from the hedge on your right as you approach a corner. Take a gap in the hedge ahead and go through a small wooded area containing springs. Continue over a stile to the right of a gate ahead. Reach a track which, if you were to stray off the right of way by going downhill on the right would lead to a field with an attractive standing stone in it. Your proper path is left, as waymarked.

4. Turn right down a lane and keep right at a junction as you descend. The tragic battlefield of Maes-Gwenllian lies across the river in front of you. Reach the main road.

5. Turn right along the main road, which has a good verge. Turn left down a lane and follow it round a very sharp right-hand bend. When the road turns left to pass Broadford Farm on your right,

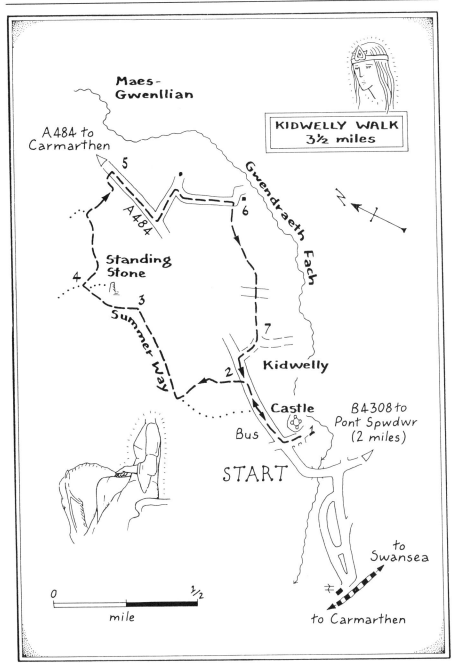

Maes-
Gwenllian

A484 to
Carmarthen

KIDWELLY WALK
3½ miles

5

Gwendraeth Fach

A484

6

Standing
Stone

4

3

Summer Way

7

2

Kidwelly

Castle

B4308 to
Pont Spwdwr
(2 miles)

Bus

START

to
Swansea

to Carmarthen

0   ½

mile

turn off the road at the preceding corner to take the old green lane on your right.

6. Go ahead up the grassy, hedged, track. Emerge through a gate onto a new road. Cross this carefully and continue through the gate opposite.

7. Reach a junction with a metalled lane and turn right uphill to a road. Turn left along the pavement back towards Kidwelly Castle.

22. caRReg cennen

Route: Carreg Cennen Castle – Llwyn-bedw – Source of Loughor – Carreg Cennen Castle.

Distance: 4 miles.

Map: OS Pathfinder 1083 Ammanford & Brynamman.

Start: Carreg Cennen Castle car park (SN 666193).

Access: Carreg Cennen Castle is four miles south-east of Llandeilo, near the village of Trapp. Trains run to Llandeilo from Swansea and Shrewsbury. The way from there by road is shown on the O.S. Landranger map no. 159 (Swansea and The Gower).

The Mysterious Tunnel of Carreg Cennen Castle

Carreg Cennen Castle occupies a spectacular hilltop site. It is in the care of CADW and has its own guidebook. Little can be said about its most mysterious feature, however. Bring a torch and explore a tunnel on its southern side. This leads to a natural cave which has yielded skeletons of prehistoric people.

At the end of the passage is a wishing well, where young ladies would throw in bent pins as they wished for a handsome husband. This limited source of water could hardly have been the reason for the passageway. Perhaps there was a deeper reason. Untold rituals may have been held in the cave, while the tunnel may point out the direction of a ley or spirit path. Perhaps there is a link with Myrddin (Merlin), although his cave is more popularly associated with nearby Dinefwr (where the castle is not open to the public because of its unsafe condition).

King Arthur's Sir Urien may have been connected with the site of the castle, while Roman coins have been found here. The views from this walk give some appreciation of this castle's especially dramatic and mystical site, even if little light can be shed on its mysterious cave.

The Walk

1. From the car park and with your back to Carreg Cennen Castle, go left back along the access lane. Turn sharply left down a lane and ignore signposted public footpaths on your left and your right. The lane bends to the left to approach a cottage.

2. Turn right before the cottage to cross a waymarked stile and take the signposted path for Llwyn-bedw. Descend to cross another waymarked stile in the bottom fence of this sloping pasture and take another stile as you descend to a small meadow. Bear slightly left to a footbridge. Cross the stream by this and continue uphill to a waymarked metalled bar stile. Keep climbing to the buildings of Llwyn-bedw.

3. Turn right, as waymarked, along Llwyn-bedw's access track. Cross a small stream and a cattle grid and continue to ford a more substantial stream and cross another cattle grid. Climb uphill with the track as it bears left. Look out for a signpost and a stile on your left.

4. Turn left over the stile to take the signposted path. Follow a firm track along the right-hand edge of this field. Cross a stream and continue, as waymarked, over a stile. Walk with the stream on your right. Follow the track to a waymark post in the fence ahead and turn left, as waymarked, across the field with the fence now on your right. Cross a stile next to a gate ahead.

5. Turn right across a field to pass an old fenced-in pit on your left. Cross a stile beside a signpost to gain access to a lane. Turn left along this. Continue over a cattle grid.

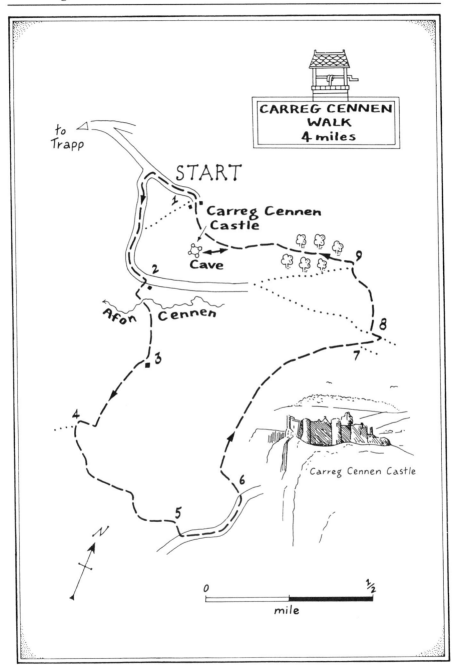

CARREG CENNEN
WALK
4 miles

to
Trapp

START

1 Carreg Cennen
Castle

Cave

9

2

Afon Cennen

8

3

7

4

Carreg Cennen Castle

6

5

N

0   ½
mile

6. When the lane bears right, fork left along the waymarked path, with a stile beside a gate. Keep to the waymarked track, heading back towards the castle, then bearing right to put the castle on your left. Walk with a fence on your left, then diverge from it to descend to a fork.

7. Bear left at the fork to descend to a lower track. Cross this lower track.

8. Cross a stile on the far side of the lower track to take the signposted path ahead. This descends to a footbridge. Cross it to continue with the stream now on your left. Take another footbridge to cross a wider stream. Go right for a few yards.

9. Turn left to follow the path uphill towards the castle and its car park.

Point 6 on the Carreg Cennen Castle walk

23. trelleck

Route: Trelleck – Harold Stones – Virtuous Well – Beacon Hill – Hen Cerrig – White Brook – Trelleck Common – Tump Terret – Trelleck.

Distance: 7 miles. Moderate.

Map: OS Outdoor Leisure 14 Wye Valley & Forest of Dean.

Start: Bus shelter (& car park), Trelleck (SO 501053).

Access: Trelleck is on the B4293 five miles south of Monmouth. Buses run from Monmouth and Chepstow. Tel. 01633 832478 for bus details.

The Leaning Stones

Christopher Houlder, in his archaeological guide to Wales, presumes that the three tall stones that now lean in various directions and are known as the Harold Stones once stood erect. Thus does the orthodox mind betray its inability to accept that our ancestors may have looked at the world through different eyes.

The Harold Stones stand in a line about 20 yards long and are 9, 12 and 15 feet high. King Harold, who lost to William the Conqueror in 1066, is said to have fought here and given his name to them, but the stones date back to the Bronze Age.

They consist of pudding stone and Trelleck is derived from the Welsh 'tri' for three and 'llech' for broad, flat, stones. Alfred Watkins recorded a legend in his *The Old Straight Track* that Jack O'Kent ('a wizard in league with the devil' who may have been Owain Glyndŵr in his final, fugitive, years) once threw the three stones from Ysgyryd Fawr, the holy hill near Abergavenny.

Wondering if my dowsing rods would indicate a ley or spirit path in the direction of Ysgyryd Fawr, I dowsed around the stones, asking only for the most important ley. My rods showed that the most important ley was being pointed out by the pronounced lean of the biggest stone. So, perhaps, they were never intended to stand erect. This most important ley led straight to the Virtuous Well, where I dowsed the same line.

The Virtuous Well, also known as St. Anne's Well, is a chalybeate spring and a wishing well. Pilgrims used to visit it, no doubt after praying at St. Nicholas' Church, outside which are an ancient preaching cross and a slab of stone known as the Druid's Altar. Near the church is Tump Terret, an ancient burial mound which had a Norman motte and bailey castle erected upon it. Terrible things will happen to anybody daring to excavate here. Take care when dowsing at the Harold Stones too. Some dowsers have felt tingling, while a couple have even been thrown back by them.

The Virtuous Well, Trelleck

The Walk

1. The bus shelter in Trelleck is across the road from the car park and caters for buses going towards Monmouth. Go right from it, in the direction of Chepstow, and soon fork right along the B4293. After 200 yards, turn left through a kissing gate to visit the Harold Stones.

2. Return to the road junction at the edge of Trelleck and bear right, as signposted for Catbrook and Tintern, ignoring a road on your right. Visit the Virtuous Well on your left before continuing to a crossroads.

3. Turn left along a lane and reach Beacon Farm on your right. Immediately after it, turn right into Beacon Hill Forest. After only 10 yards, bear right off the forest track to climb steeply with a footpath.

4. Go ahead at a path junction and walk between plantations of conifers. Maintain this direction by going ahead across firm tracks.

5. Reach a fork beneath a tall pine tree and take the path bearing left to pass the tree on your right. Emerge from the forest, ignoring a signposted footpath to Manorside on your left. Go ahead along a lane and descend to a telephone box.

6. Cross a road to continue downhill with the lane and reach a fork at the head of a green. Bear left to a house called Hen Cerrig.

7. Take the path which bears left down through woodland to Whitebrook.

8. Turn left along the road up the wooded valley, soon passing a telephone box on your left.

9. Turn left up a lane to a higher road. Cross it and take the signposted bridleway ahead to Warren's Road. This leads to a firm forest track. Go straight ahead with it until the track swings left.

10. Go straight ahead along the waymarked public bridleway (a blue arrow). Converge with a path coming sharply from your left. Go ahead as waymarked, ignoring a forest ride on your right. Continue across a forest track.

11. The waymarked route leads ahead through an avenue of trees. Emerge on a road and cross it to continue over a stile way-marked with a yellow arrow and signposted for Greenway Lane. The enclosed path leads to a corner of a field. Go ahead along its right-hand edge. Cross a stile in the corner and bear left, as waymarked, to go down steps to a road.

12. Turn right down the road and pass Greenway Cottage on your right. Reach the B4293 at a bus stop near the Lion Inn, Trelleck.

13. Turn right to pass St. Nicholas' Church on your left and take the signposted public footpath to Tump Terret on your left. Go ahead over a waymarked stile and along the left-hand edge of a field. Leave this by a step stile followed by a ladder stile in the next corner. Ignore another stile on your right. Bear left to pass Tump Terret's old mound and reach a stile in the far corner. Cross it and turn right through the farmyard, then turn left down the access lane to reach the main road near the bus shelter and the car park.

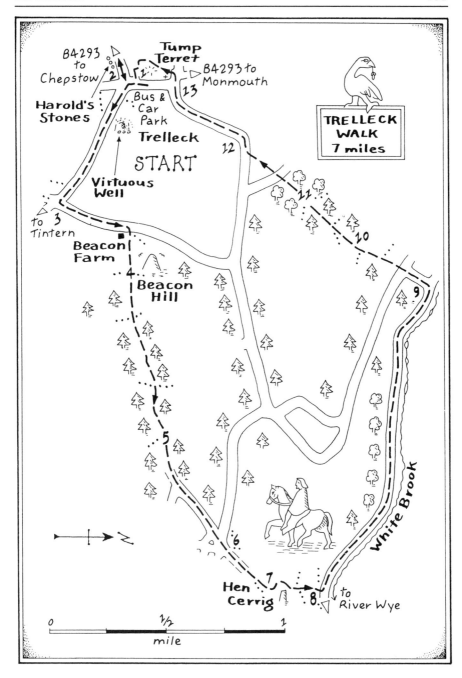

B4293
to
Chepstow

Tump
Terret

B4293 to
Monmouth

13

Harold's
Stones

Bus &
Car
Park

Trelleck

START

12

TRELLECK
WALK
7 miles

Virtuous
Well

to 3
Tintern

11

Beacon
Farm

10

4

9

Beacon
Hill

5

White Brook

6

Hen
Cerrig

7

8

to
River Wye

N

0   ½   1

mile

24. Ogmore

Route: St. Bride's Major – Pant Mari Flanders – Pant y Cwteri – Ogmore Castle – St. Bride's Major.

Distance: 4 miles. Moderate.

Map: OS Pathfinder 1163 Bridgend (South) and Porthcawl.

Start: The *redundant* bus shelter near the village shop and the car park for the Fox & Hounds pub at the northern end of St. Bride's Major – the current bus shelter is at the southern end of the village (SS 895750).

Access: St. Bride's Major is at the junction of the B4524 and the B4265 four miles south of Bridgend, where there is a railway station. Bus no. 145 stops here on the way between Bridgend and Llantwit Major (tel. 01222 820626 for details).

Ogmore

The name of the village at the start of this walk and the dedication of its church to St. Bridget indicate that this is White Goddess territory. This route also passes a finely preserved holy well at Pant Mari Flanders. It comes as no surprise, therefore, to discover the story of the white lady at Ogmore Castle. One night she appeared to a man and led him up the castle tower and asked him to lift a stone in its floor. This was raised to reveal a treasure of gold coins in a cauldron. He took half of them, as directed by the white lady, leaving the rest under the replaced stone. Tempted to return for more gold later, he was met by the white lady and accused of theft. He soon fell ill and confessed the truth before dying.

To die without passing on knowledge of hidden treasure would be to risk torment after death, unless the treasure could be returned to its rightful owner or thrown downstream into a river. Barbara, the wife of a tailor from Llantwit Major, agreed to appease her mother-in-law's ghost by throwing some money into the river at Ogmore. She made the mistake of throwing it upstream, however, which caused many more years of trouble from the ghost.

Ogmore Castle was built by William de Londres as part of the Norman plan to control the Vale of Glamorgan in the 12th century. His daughter once pleaded for the life of a handsome Welshman caught poaching on her father's land. Being her birthday, she was granted her wish and allowed to walk barefoot before sunset to mark out common ground, now a golf course south of the castle, where the Welsh would be entitled to hunt.

Ogmore Castle

The Walk

1. Face the redundant bus shelter near the village shop in St. Bride's Major, go right, then turn left towards St. Bridget's Church. Ignore Heol-yr-Ysgol bearing left and fork right to pass the church on your left. Pass Lon-yr-Eglwys on your left. Go ahead over a cattle grid and fork left.

2. Go ahead over a metal bar stile in the wall to the left of a gate across the track. Walk along the right-hand edge of a field, passing Tyn-y-caeau on your right. Cross another bar stile in the corner ahead to continue along the left-hand edges of fields. Go ahead over a stile to the left of a gate, cross a firm track and walk with a fence on your right to a signpost near a bend in the road on your left. Bear right beside the fence on your right. Ignore a fenced track going right.

3. When the fence on your right turns right, go ahead towards an old, broken wall and turn right down a dry valley. Pass a covered holy well on your right and fork right down a dry valley with trees clothing the slope away to your left.

4. Turn right along the road, with the river away to your left. Reach a pub called The Pelican on your right. Turn left down the access lane to Ogmore Castle.

5. Retrace your steps to The Pelican, pass the pub on your left and turn left up the lane to the golf course. Ignore a signposted bridleway on your right and bear left with the lane to pass above the back of the pub. Climb to where the lane turns right to the golf clubhouse and the wall on your left ends.

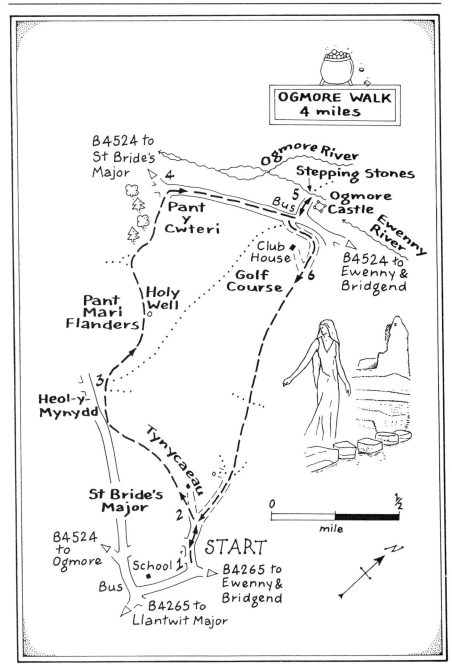

6. Go straight ahead along the path between gorse bushes. Eventually reach a corner formed by two hedges and go ahead with a hedge, becoming a fence, on your right. Reach a signpost for the bridleway you have just traversed at the start of a lane and go ahead along this lane. Retrace your steps over the cattle grid, pass the church on your right and return to the redundant bus shelter at the start of this walk.

25. Llantrisant

Route: Talbot Green – Y Graig – Llantrisant – Caeau'r llan – Dan Caerlan – Llantrisant – Heol Sticil y Beddau – Talbot Green.

Distance: 3½ miles. Moderate.

Map: OS Pathfinder 1148 Pontypridd (South) and Caerphilly.

Start: Bus station (& car park), Talbot Green (ST 041830).

Access: Talbot Green is at the junction of the A4119 (from Cardiff to Tonypandy) and the A473 (from Bridgend to Pontypridd), about three miles north of junction 34 on the M4. Buses run from Cardiff, Pontypridd, Bridgend and Tonypandy. Tel. 01222 820626 for bus details.

A Latterday Druid

Reverence for nature, a vegetarian diet, a belief in free love and political radicalism all found an exponent in the striking figure whose statue now dominates the Bullring of Llantrisant. Dr. William Price was an extraordinary, idiosyncratic, character. Born in 1800 as the son of an Anglican clergyman, he knew himself to be the reincarnation of a druid.

Unrestricted by the dogma of the written word, he moved with the spirit. As a qualified surgeon, he treated the poor for free, then charged the rich appropriately. He concentrated on causes, not symptoms, in the Nature Cure tradition and insisted that his patients stopped smoking. Unmarried mothers knew to turn to him for aid.

Involved in the Chartist movement, he had to seek sanctuary in France for seven years after the failure of the Chartist riots in 1839. No stranger to the courts, he defended himself fearlessly. He was a firm believer in cremation, declaring that good land was wasted and polluted by the burial of corpses.

Tragically, he had to put his belief into effect when his baby son, Iesu (Jesus) died in 1884, aged five months. He had fathered the child on a girl, Gwenllian Llewellyn, less than a third of his age. Spotted cremating the body on the hilltop of Caeau'r llan, he was arrested, despite Gwenllian's attempt to hold off interferers with a gun. Charged with the illegal disposal of a body, he conducted his own defence and was found not guilty.

He went ahead with the cremation of Iesu, then fathered a second son called Iesu and a daughter, Penelopen, before his own death and cremation in 1893. Over 20,000 ticket-holders gathered on Caeau'r llan to witness the latter, now legal, event.

There is no right of way up Caeau'r llan, so this route encircles the hill. When in Llantrisant's Bullring, put your back to the statue of Dr. Price and look ahead to the hilltop of Caeau'r llan, with the house near the summit being a former home of Dr. Price. Visit an exhibition in the Model House, behind the statue. This is now a craft and design visitor centre but was once a chemist's owned by Lord (Dr.) David Owen's great grandfather.

The Royal Mint has a display in the Model House, although no free samples are available. The kingdom's money is all minted in an industrial estate just to the north of Llantrisant. This old town is certainly not 'the hole with the mint in it', however. Old cobbled alleys bless it with the charm of an age when it stood on the border between the rich agricultural Vale of Glamorgan and the wilder hills (and coalfields) to the north. The view from the bracken-covered slopes of Y Graig may include modern roads, shopping centres, housing and industrial estates, but old Llantrisant rises above all that.

The church is dedicated to the three saints whose coming together here in the sixth century gave the town its name (Llantrisant means 'the sacred enclosure of three saints'). They were Illtyd, Gwynno and Dyfodwg. A stained glass window in the church depicts Jesus Christ without a beard. The Normans built a castle at this strategic spot and one tower of it (Twr-y-Gigfran, meaning 'tower of the raven') survives. Edward II was imprisoned here shortly before his murder in 1326, having been captured at Pant-y-Brad (the Hollow of Treason), grid ref. ST 024877. The local rugby team is still called the 'black army' after the company of archers who went from here to help Edward III at the Battle of Crecy.

Returning to Talbot Green by way of Zoar Chapel, notice the plaque on the side of it, commemorating the legalisation of cremation. The chapel was formerly a house occupied by Dr. Price and his daughter, Penelopen, unveiled the plaque in 1947. The old lane known as Heol Sticil y Beddau (the lane with the stile to the graveyard) may be a spirit path or ley. It is aligned with the summit of Caeau'r llan, giving a clue as to why the latterday druid chose that spot to cremate his dead son.

Statue of Dr William Price, Llantrisant

The Walk

1. There is a car park above Talbot Green's bus station, which slopes down to the A473 road. Go right from the bus station to walk uphill past public toilets and the car park on your right. Soon pass Maes y Rhedyn on your left, then the Hand and Squirrel pub on your right. Pass Danygraig Drive on your right and come to a junction with the Ely Valley Road. Cross this to reach public footpath signposts at the foot of Y Graig, the hillside facing you.

2. Don't take the footpath signposted as going left. Climb uphill and bear right to a path junction. Go right with a path contouring around the hillside. Turn sharply left at the next junction and follow the uphill path to a waymark post for the Ridgeway Walk at a higher path junction.

3. Turn left with the waymarked Ridgeway Walk (a 21 mile route between Mynydd y Gaer and Caerphilly Common). Soon leave it by forking right uphill. Reach the fence at the top of the ridge and turn sharply right to walk along the crest of the ridge to a roofless tower which was an old windmill. Bonfires are lit here on special occasions, so it may be an old beacon site. Leave the fence before it forms a corner with a fence ahead. Descend to walk with the lower fence on your left and come to houses on your left. Another path comes sharply from the right to converge with yours. Go ahead along an enclosed path.

4. Emerge from Heol-y-Graig and go uphill past a school on your left. Turn right to take a path through the churchyard, passing the church on your left and going out through a gate on the far side. Cross the cobbled land of Yr Allt and take the path ahead to see the remains of the castle.

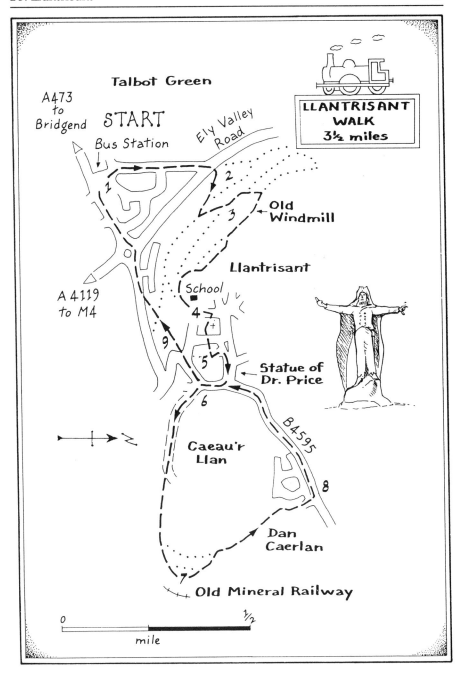

Talbot Green

A473
to
Bridgend START

Bus Station

Ely Valley Road

LLANTRISANT
WALK
3½ miles

2

3 Old
Windmill

A 4119
to M4

Llantrisant

School

4

9

5

Statue of
Dr. Price

6

B4595

Caeau'r
Llan

8

Dan
Caerlan

7 Old Mineral Railway

0   ½
mile

5. Turn left to pass the town hall on your right and go right when you come to a lane. This takes you down to the Model House, on your left, with the statue of Dr. Price in front of it, in the Bullring. Go ahead to descend past the Cross Keys pub on your left. Turn right at the next junction. When level with the Penfel and Trinity Presbyterian Church on your right, turn left down a lane.

6. Pass the Old Fox Stables on your left, ignore a lane forking right and go straight ahead along a private road (but public footpath). Caeau'r Ilan is above on your left. When the metalled lane ends, fork slightly right along the hedged path which is waymarked as forming part of the Ridgeway Walk. The path soon diverges from the descending hedge on your right and contours around the hill at the foot of a wooded slope on your left. Go ahead, as waymarked, through a kissing gate, go down open pasture to steps in its bottom corner. These lead to an old mineral railway line.

7. Turn sharply left before the old railway and climb to a waymarked path junction beneath an oak tree. Bear right to climb to a higher path and bear right along this, passing the bracken-covered hillside sloping upwards on your left. Continue to the housing estate at Dan Caerlan and bear right along a track past the backs of the houses to emerge at the B4595 road.

8. Go left, with the pavement of an estate road which runs parallel to the B4595, pass a bus stop, then along a pavement beside the B4595. Pass the Castle Inn on your right, then the rugby ground (where the 'black army' plays). Continue past the Cross Keys pub on your right and retrace your steps through Llantrisant to the Penfel and Trinity Presbyterian Church on your right. Pass the Wheatsheaf pub on your left, ignore Church

Street forking on your right, come to a hairpin bend on your left and look for the plaque on the side of Zoar Chapel on your right.

9. Retrace your steps from Zoar Chapel uphill for 30 yards and turn sharply left to pass above Zoar Chapel on your left along Heol Sticil y Beddau (the lane with the stile to the graveyard). Go down this cobbled lane, ignoring turnings, to the main road and turn right to the roundabout. Go ahead along the pavement of the A473, passing Danygraig Drive on your right, to return to the bus station and car park at Talbot Green, on your right.

26. castell coch

Route: Cardiff Castle – Llandaff Cathedral – Melingriffith Water Pump – Tongwynlais – Castell Coch – Tongwynlais (bus back to Cardiff).

Distance: 7½ miles (linear). Easy.

Map: OS Pathfinder 1148 Pontypridd (South) and Caerphilly and 1165 Cardiff and Penarth.

Start: Cardiff Castle (ST 181765).

Access: Cardiff Castle is in the centre of Cardiff, near the railway and bus stations. Bus no. 136 goes direct from Castell Coch to Cardiff, otherwise return to Cardiff by bus from Tongwynlais (nos. 26,132 and X5).

Castell Coch

The official CADW guidebook will tell you how the third Marquis of Bute rebuilt Castell Coch in the late 19th century. There was a castle here long before then, however, with a tale of hidden treasure guarded by two eagles. This was said to be in an underground passage linking Castell Coch with Cardiff Castle. Around 1800, it is said that a party of men tried to take this treasure, using pistols which fired silver bullets blessed by a priest to kill the guardian eagles. They did not succeed, so presumably it is still there.

Is the 'underground passage' a folk memory of a ley? Several leys, or spirit paths, do converge on Castell Coch, including one from Cardiff Castle. Perhaps the 'treasure' was a dream of the future wealth of this area. The third Marquis of Bute was reputed to be the richest man in the world. Cardiff became the prosperous port which exported the coal mined from his estates.

The Marquis also had mystical interests and it is significant that the banqueting hall at Castell Coch is adorned by a statue of King Lucius. At Winchester in A.D. 156, Lucius proclaimed Christianity as the national faith of Britain, thus making Britain the first Christian nation. He was a great-grandson of King Arviragus of the Silures who had granted the twelve hides of Glastonbury to Joseph of Arimathea. We are very close here to the mystery of this sceptre'd isle. As Taliesin declared in the sixth century: 'Christ, the Word from the beginning, was from the beginning our teacher, and we never lost His teaching. Christianity was a new thing in Asia, but there never was a time when the Druids of Britain held not its doctrines.'

Start at Cardiff Castle

This route from the old Roman fort of Cardiff Castle also brings the pilgrim to Llandaff Cathedral. Legend has it that Shakespeare's King Lear (Llyr, father of Bran) founded the first Christian church in Wales at Llandaff. Meurig, the father of King Arthur, is buried near the altar on the right-hand side of God. St. Teilo lies on the south side opposite St. Dyfrig, who crowned Arthur and whose remains were brought here from Bardsey for reburial in 1120.

The Walk

1. Face the main entrance to Cardiff Castle and go right, with the castle on your left. Turn left up Kingsway and, when level with Boulevard de Nantes across the road on your right, turn left into Bute Park. Pass the northern wall of the castle on your left and tennis courts on your right. Go ahead across a bridge over the Dock Feeder Canal. Continue to the River Taff.

2. Turn right to walk with the River Taff on your left. Keep to the narrow, riverside, path when the main path bears right. Pass Blackweir on your left. Pass under the bridge which carries Western Avenue across the river.

3. Immediately after going under the bridge, go up stairs and cross the river by the bridge. Turn right through a gate to follow the waymarked Taff Valley Heritage Trail, keeping the river on your right.

4. Turn sharply left to cross playing fields and reach Llandaff Cathedral. Continue by retracing your steps, going right from the cathedral. Turn left to take the path inside woodland. Pass Llandaff Weir on your right. Follow the path up to a road on your left.

5. Go right and soon bear right down a path back towards the river. This path leads back to the road. Fork right to cross a bridge over the river.

6. Go down steps on your right to join the riverside path. Turn right to pass under the bridge and continue with the river on your left and Hailey Park on your right. Turn right to take the path across this park to a road. Go left to follow Ty-Mawr Road under a railway bridge. Reach the Melingriffith Water Pump on your left.

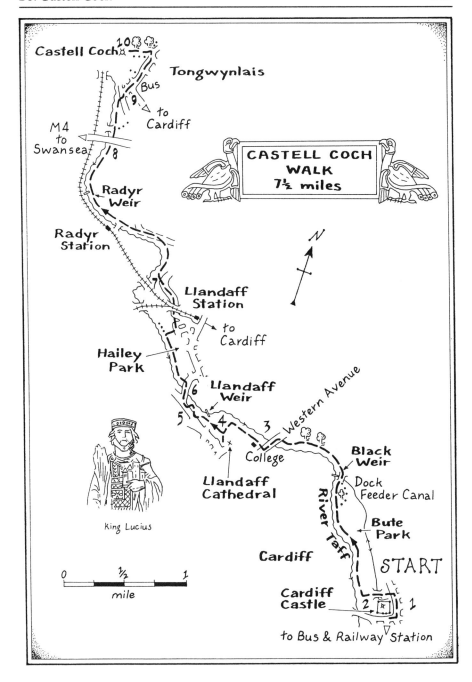

Castell Coch

10 Tongwynlais

Bus

9

to Cardiff

M4 to Swansea

8

Radyr Weir

Radyr Station

CASTELL COCH
WALK
7½ miles

N

Llandaff Station

to Cardiff

Hailey Park

Llandaff Weir

6

5

4

3

Western Avenue

College

Llandaff Cathedral

Black Weir

Dock Feeder Canal

King Lucius

Bute Park

River Taff

Cardiff

START

0   ½   1
mile

Cardiff Castle

2

1

to Bus & Railway Station

7. Follow the signposted route for pedestrians to Castell Coch, turning left off Ty-Mawr Road. Soon bear left again to come beside the River Taff, on your left. Continue along the course of an old tramway, now a lane. Pass a footbridge spanning the river on your left (giving access to Radyr Station), then pass Radyr Weir.

8. Take the signposted route under the bridge which carries the M4. Ignore a footbridge across the river on your left. Continue through kissing gates, then bear right, as waymarked, to pass under the A470 and reach Tongwynlais.

9. Go ahead with the waymarked Taff Valley Heritage Trail. Pass the Lewis Arms on your left, pass a golf course on your left and reach the drive to Castell Coch. Bear left up it, through woodland, to the castle.

10. Retrace your steps down to Tongwynlais for buses back to Cardiff.

27. tresilian caoe

Route: Llantwit Major – Tresilian Bay – Cwm Col-huw – Llantwit Major.

Distance: 4 miles.

Map: O.S. Pathfinder 1163 Bridgend (South) and Porthcawl

Start: Llantwit Major Tourist Information Centre (SS 966687).

Access: Llantwit Major is at the junction of the B4265 and the B4270 about 15 miles south-west of Cardiff. Buses run here from all parts of Glamorgan. Telephone 01222 873252 for details.

Tresilian Cave

The big cave with the arch in its roof at the southernmost end of the western side of Tresilian Bay should be approached at low tide. It is a very romantic spot because lovers would come here to throw a pebble through the arch. It had to fall on the other side cleanly without having touched either the roof of the cave or the beam of the arch. Prospective husbands no doubt went secretly to gain expertise in this feat before coming with their loved one, for if the wedding was to take place within the year the suitor must succeed with the first throw. If it took a second throw, the wedding would be delayed until the second year and so on. Young couples would sometimes be married in the cave. Prince Silian, who was the local ruler in the time of the Romans, must have been a great lover, because the cave is named after him, although he became an early Christian saint.

Christianity flourished at nearby Llantwit Major in the sixth century when St. Illtud's college educated men such as St. Samson, who became Archbishop of Dol, St. Gildas, St. David and Taliesin. St. Illtud was a cousin of King Arthur and convincing evidence for locating Arthur in South Wales (before he ended his days in Brittany) is the Samson Stone, with its reference to Arthmael (Arthur), kept at the back of St. Illtud's Church.

Llantwit Major's history dates back to even more stirring times because it is said that the very first church here was founded by St. Eurgain, who met the early Christians such as St. Peter and St. Paul when they sought refuge at the palace-in-exile at Rome of her father, Caractacus. The Romans had a harbour in Cwm Col-huw, which is where St. Illtud probably disembarked after travelling here from Britanny. As well as being a saint and a great educator, Illtud was famous for being one of King Arthur's knights.

Looking across Tresilian Bay to the mouth of the cave

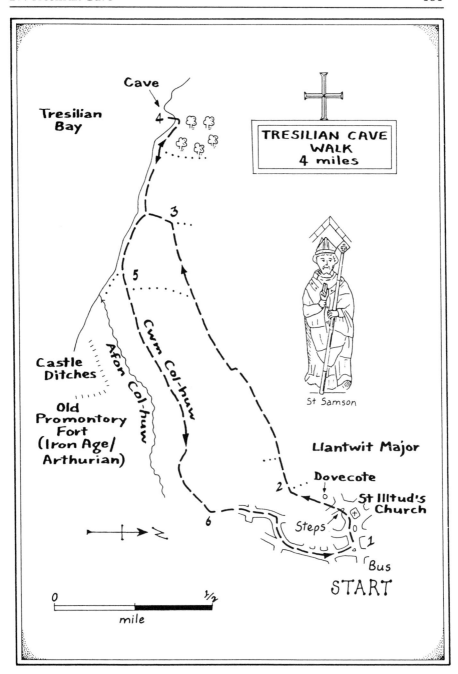

Cave

Tresilian
Bay

4

TRESILIAN CAVE
WALK
4 miles

3

5

Cwm Col-huw

Castle
Ditches

Afon Col-huw

St Samson

Old
Promontory
Fort
(Iron Age/
Arthurian)

Llantwit Major

Dovecote

2

St Illtud's
Church

N

Steps

1

6

Bus

START

0   ½
mile

The Walk

1. Facing the Tourist Information Centre, go right along Church Street to St. Illtud's Church. Leave by the gate at the far end of the churchyard, with the church on your right, and go left. Take the steps going up on your right. Turn left at the top of them and reach a stone stile on your right which gives access to a field containing a dovecote. Pass this on your right as you cross the field diagonally to a stone stile in the far left-hand corner.

2. Cross the stile and go ahead along Church Lane, a hedged track which may have a muddy surface. Emerge over a stone stile ahead and continue towards the Bristol Channel along the left-hand edge of a field.

3. Go ahead over a stile in the corner of the field and immediately turn left over a stone stile with metal bars. Continue to the coast path. Turn right to walk above the sea on your left and reach Tresilian Bay, with the romantic cave at the southern-most point of its western side (don't be fooled by a smaller cave halfway along the western side).

4. Retrace your steps from Tresilian Bay, with the sea now on your right. Continue to Cwm Col-huw, where the Afon Col-huw flows towards the Bristol Channel.

5. Take the inland path, climbing steps and keeping above the valley of the river on your right. The path becomes a track which eventually heads down to old farm buildings, where you cross a stile beside a gate.

6. Turn left along a lane and head into Llantwit Major. Follow the lane as it crosses a stream on your right. Pass White House Close on your left. Reach the end of Flanders Road and turn left at a road junction, opposite a letterbox. Pass Italian Joe's Restaurant on your left, then bear left at a fork to pass the Old Swan Inn on your right. The car park is opposite this and the Tourist Information Centre ahead on your left.

Walking notes

Use these pages to record your walks – or any mysterious happenings!

Walking notes

Walking notes

We publish guides to individual towns, plus books on walking and cycling in the great out-doors throughout England and Wales. This is a recent selection:

Walking & Cycling in Wales

WELSH WALKS: Dolgellau /Cambrian Coast – L. Main & M. Perrott *(£5.95)*

WELSH WALKS: Aberystwyth & District – L. Main & M. Perrott *(£5.95)*

GREAT WALKS FROM WELSH RAILWAYS – Les Lumsdon & Colin Speakman *(£4.95)*

RAMBLES IN NORTH WALES – Roger Redfern *(£6.95)*

CHALLENGING WALKS: NW England & N Wales – Ron Astley *(£7.95)*

PUB WALKS IN SNOWDONIA – Laurence Main *(£6.95)*

BEST PUB WALKS AROUND CHESTER & THE DEE VALLEY – John Haywood *(£6.95)*

BEST PUB WALKS IN GWENT – Les Lumsdon *(£6.95)*

PUB WALKS IN POWYS – Les Lumsdon & Chris Rushton *(£6.95)*

BEST PUB WALKS IN PEMBROKESHIRE – Laurence Main *(£6.95)*

CYCLING IN SOUTH WALES – Rosemary Evans *(£7.95)*

CYCLING IN NORTH WALES – Philip Routledge *(£7.95) ... available 1996*

Other destinations

FIFTY CLASSIC WALKS IN THE PENNINES – Terry Marsh *(£8.95)*

YORKSHIRE: a walk around my county – Tony Whittaker *(£7.95)*

HERITAGE WALKS IN THE PEAK DISTRICT – Clive Price *(£6.95)*

EAST CHESHIRE WALKS – Graham Beech *(£5.95)*

WEST CHESHIRE WALKS – Jen Darling *(£5.95)*

WEST PENNINE WALKS – Mike Cresswell *(£5.95)*

RAMBLES AROUND MANCHESTER – Mike Cresswell *(£5.95)*

YORKSHIRE DALES WALKING: On The Level – Norman Buckley *(£6.95)*

100 LAKE DISTRICT HILL WALKS – Gordon Brown *(£7.95)*

THE LAKELAND SUMMITS – Tim Synge *(£7.95)*

LAKELAND ROCKY RAMBLES: Geology beneath your feet – Brian Lynas *(£9.95)*

FULL DAYS ON THE FELLS: Challenging Walks – Adrian Dixon *(£7.95)*

PUB WALKS IN THE LAKE DISTRICT – Neil Coates *(£6.95)*

LAKELAND WALKING, ON THE LEVEL – Norman Buckley *(£6.95)*
MOSTLY DOWNHILL: LEISURELY WALKS, LAKE DISTRICT – Alan Pears *(£6.95)*
TEA SHOP WALKS IN THE LAKE DISTRICT – Norman Buckley *(£6.95)*

Cycling

CYCLE UK! The essential guide to leisure cycling – Les Lumsdon *(£9.95)*
OFF-BEAT CYCLING IN THE PEAK DISTRICT – Clive Smith *(£6.95)*
MORE OFF-BEAT CYCLING IN THE PEAK DISTRICT – Clive Smith *(£6.95)*
50 BEST CYCLE RIDES IN CHESHIRE – edited by Graham Beech *(£7.95)*
CYCLING IN THE COTSWOLDS – Stephen Hill *(£6.95)*
CYCLING IN THE CHILTERNS – Henry Tindell *(£7.95)*
CYCLING IN THE LAKE DISTRICT – John Wood *(£7.95)*
CYCLING IN LINCOLNSHIRE – Penny & Bill Howe *(£7.95)*
CYCLING IN NOTTINGHAMSHIRE – Penny & Bill Howe *(£7.95)*
CYCLING IN STAFFORDSHIRE – Linda Wain *(£7.95)*
CYCLING IN THE WEST COUNTRY – Helen Stephenson *(£7.95)*

Sport

RED FEVER: from Rochdale to Rio as 'United' supporters – Steve Donoghue *(£7.95)*
UNITED WE STOOD: unofficial history of the Ferguson years – Richard Kurt *(£6.95)*
MANCHESTER CITY: Moments to Remember – John Creighton *(£9.95)*
AN A TO Z OF MANCHESTER CITY – Dean Hayes *(£6.95)*

Heritage

SECRET YORK: walks within the city walls – Les Pierce *(£6.95)*
CHILLING TRUE TALES OF OLD LANCASHIRE – Keith Johnson *(£6.95)*
WESTON-SUPER-MARE: the sands of time – Anthony Keyes *(£6.95)*